WHISPERED HARMONY

Empower Your Bonds, Transform Your Life

Unleashing the Art of Peaceful Correspondence

ANNETTE A. WALLACE

1

Table of Contents

INTRODUCTION

BUILDING EXTENSIONS OF UNDERSTANDING

In a world frequently set apart by errors, clashes, and disengagement, the force of correspondence can't be undervalued. Our words can possibly recuperate wounds, span partitions, and develop significant associations among people and networks. In any case, unreasonably frequently, our correspondence misses the mark, prompting disappointment, outrage, and viciousness.

Inside the pages of this book, we will dive into the fundamental standards and functional uses of Peaceful Correspondence. We will uncover the force of language in molding our connections and investigate how Peaceful Correspondence can assist us with changing struggles into open doors for development and association.

Part I: Figuring out Peaceful Correspondence

In this part, we establish the groundwork for our investigation of Peaceful Correspondence. We will find the power it holds and changing our lives and connections with others potential.

The Force of Peaceful Correspondence

We will investigate the significant effect of Peaceful Correspondence on cultivating grasping, settling clashes, and building scaffolds of association. This part will give bits of knowledge into the extraordinary capability of peaceful correspondence

Language and Connections

Language assumes a urgent part in our connections. In this section, we will dig into the manners by which language shapes our connections, both decidedly and adversely. We will uncover the keys to developing cognizant and caring correspondence.

Changing Clash with Peacefulness

Struggle is a characteristic piece of human connections. Nonetheless, with the apparatuses of Peaceful Correspondence, we can change clashes into open doors for development and understanding. This part will investigate the groundbreaking capability of peacefulness in settling clashes calmly.

Noticing, Feeling, and Requiring

In this segment, we dig into the center parts of Peaceful Correspondence: seeing without judgment, communicating sentiments legitimately, and recognizing basic requirements.

Creating mindfulness

Mindfulness is the most vital move toward compelling correspondence. We will investigate practices and strategies that develop mindfulness and the capacity to notice ourselves as well as other people without judgment.

Noticing versus Assessing

Recognizing perceptions and assessments is critical in Peaceful Correspondence. In this section, we will figure out how to move from evaluative language to genuine perceptions, empowering more clear and more empathic correspondence.

Communicating Sentiments and Distinguishing Needs

Sentiments and necessities lie at the center of our human experience. We will find how to recognize and communicate our sentiments legitimately, while at the same time uncovering the fundamental necessities that drive our feelings.

Making Sympathetic Solicitations

In this part, we investigate the craft of making sympathetic solicitations that honor our requirements and encourage understanding and cooperation.

Figuring out Successful Solicitations

Powerful demands are the foundation of Peaceful Correspondence. This section will direct us in figuring out clear, significant solicitations that regard the requirements and upsides of all gatherings included.

Positive and Explicit Language

The words we pick shape our world. We will investigate the significance of positive and explicit language in establishing a correspondence climate that cultivates compassion, association, and understanding.

Demands in Connections

Expanding on the standards canvassed in past parts, we will apply the craft of sympathetic solicitations to our connections. We will find how to support trust, resolve clashes, and develop profound association through peaceful correspondence.

Part II: Applying Peaceful Correspondence in Different Life Settings

In this part, we investigate the reasonable utilizations of Peaceful Correspondence in various everyday issues, including connections, nurturing, the working environment, and our own taking care of oneself.

Peaceful Correspondence in Connections
We will dive into how Peaceful Correspondence can upgrade our connections, sustaining trust, closeness, and genuine association with our friends and family.

Peaceful Correspondence in Nurturing
Nurturing presents remarkable difficulties where correspondence assumes an essential part. This part will investigate how Peaceful Correspondence can uphold guardians in cultivating compassion, settling clashes, and empowering close to home advancement in their kids.

Peaceful Correspondence in the Working environment
Working environment elements can be changed through Peaceful Correspondence. We will investigate how PC can improve relational abilities, resolve clashes, and encourage joint effort and compassion among associates.

PART III: Applying Peaceful Correspondence in Day to day existence

Peaceful Correspondence stretches out past unambiguous settings. In this section, we will investigate how we can apply PC standards to develop self-empathy, change self-analysis, and support profound prosperity in our day to day routines.

As we proceed with our investigation of Peaceful Correspondence, we perceive that the ability to change our reality exists in every one of us. By coordinating the standards and practices of PC into our lives, we can cultivate humane correspondence, resolve clashes calmly, and construct amicable connections and networks.

May this book act as an aide, enlightening the way of Peaceful Correspondence and rousing us to construct extensions of figuring out, sympathy, and association in our own lives and in our general surroundings.

PART 1

UNDERSTANDING PEACEFUL CORRESPONDENCE

CHAPTER 1 :

The Force Of Peaceful Correspondence

In a world loaded up with struggle and conflict, the force of peaceful correspondence remains as an encouraging sign. Peaceful correspondence, frequently shortened as (PC), is a way to deal with relational correspondence that underscores sympathy, understanding, and empathy. PC has since earned far reaching respect for its capacity to change connections, cultivate harmony, and make enduring change. This part investigates the pitch of peaceful correspondence and its gigantic ability to reshape our co operations, mend profound injuries, and assemble amicable associations.

Grasping Peaceful Correspondence:

At its center, peaceful correspondence is a course of legitimate articulation and empathic tuning in. It is based upon the crucial conviction that all people have the limit with respect to empathy and the longing to satisfy their necessities. PC trains us to see without judgment, distinguish our sentiments and necessities, articulate our thoughts self-assuredly, and look for understanding from others. By taking part in this merciful methodology, we can defeat boundaries, break down clashes, and develop further associations.

The Four Parts of Peaceful Correspondence:
Peaceful correspondence comprises four key parts that structure the groundwork of the cycle. These parts are:

1. Perception: The most important phase in peaceful correspondence is the act of mentioning objective facts without assessment or judgment. By portraying realities as opposed to deciphering or naming, we make a shared view for understanding.

2. Sentiments: Distinguishing and communicating our sentiments is a significant part of PC. Recognizing our feelings and perceiving their association with our requirements empowers us to impart all the more truly and truly.

3. Needs: Peaceful correspondence perceives that all people have general requirements for things like love, security, regard, and independence. Understanding and articulating our necessities assists us with interfacing with others on a more profound level and track down commonly fulfilling arrangements.

4. Demands: The last part of PC includes clarifying, explicit, and possible solicitations. By zeroing in on substantial activities that can satisfy our necessities, we set out open doors for cooperation and association.

THE FORCE OF SYMPATHY AND ASSOCIATION

One of the most groundbreaking parts of peaceful correspondence is its accentuation on sympathy and association. PC welcomes us to step into the shoes of others, listen profoundly to their sentiments and needs, and answer with understanding and empathy. Through empathic tuning in, we make a place of refuge for open discourse, encouraging trust and closeness in our connections. This capacity to identify interfaces on a significant level has the ability to recuperate close to home injuries, resolve clashes, and construct spans across different networks.

Transforming Conflict with Peaceful Correspondence

Struggle is an unavoidable piece of human communication, however PC offers a way towards a tranquil goal. By reevaluating struggle as a chance for understanding and development, peaceful correspondence empowers us to change ill-disposed elements into agreeable critical thinking. Through undivided attention, communicating our necessities and sentiments, and looking for commonly helpful arrangements, we can break free from horrendous examples and make a more amicable world.

Peaceful Correspondence in Regular day to day existence:

While peaceful correspondence is frequently connected with settling clashes for a bigger scope, its standards can be applied to our regular communications too. PCs can upgrade our associations with relatives, companions, partners, and even outsiders. By cultivating sympathy, undivided attention, and genuine articulation, we establish a caring climate where understanding and association thrive.

The Effect of Peaceful Correspondence

The effect of peaceful correspondence stretches out a long way past individual connections. At the point when applied for a bigger scope, PC can possibly encourage social change, advance equity, and make more tranquil social orders. By developing sympathy and understanding, people can challenge abusive frameworks, advocate for correspondence, and work towards settling cultural struggles.

The force of peaceful correspondence lies in its capacity to change our associations, recuperate profound injuries, and construct amicable associations. By embracing the standards of perception, sentiments, needs, and demands, we can develop sympathy, understanding, and empathy in our connections. Peaceful correspondence furnishes us with an integral asset to determine clashes, cultivate harmony, and make enduring change in both individual and cultural settings. As we leave on this excursion of investigating peaceful correspondence, we open ourselves to an existence where understanding and association beat dissension and savagery.

LANGUAGE AND CONNECTIONS:

Language assumes a central part in forming our connections. It is through language that we offer our viewpoints, feelings, needs, and wants to other people. The nature of our language and correspondence straightforwardly influences the profundity of our associations and the degree of understanding we can accomplish with people around us. In this section, we will investigate the mind boggling association among language and connections, and how Peaceful Correspondence (PC) can assist us with utilizing language all the more to make further associations, resolve clashes, and cultivate understanding.

The Force of Words

Words have colossal power. They can move, mend, and unite individuals, however they can likewise twist, partition, and make obstructions. The manner in which we express ourselves, the tone we use, and the aim behind our correspondence fundamentally influence the nature of our connections. Peaceful Correspondence perceives the force of words and underscores involving language in a manner that advances compassion, understanding, and association.

Careful Correspondence

Peaceful Correspondence urges us to develop care in our correspondence. Careful correspondence includes monitoring our contemplations, feelings, and goals prior to talking. It expects us to stop, reflect, and express ourselves intentionally. By rehearsing careful correspondence, we can stay away from incautious responses, answer with compassion, and cultivate more credible and significant associations with others.

Empathic Tuning in

Successful correspondence isn't just about talking; it additionally includes tuning in. Empathic listening is a foundation of Peaceful Correspondence. It expects us to completely draw in with the speaker, suspend judgment, and look to figure out the sentiments and necessities behind their words. Empathic listening permits us to make a place of refuge for open exchange, develop our connections, and encourage shared understanding.

Genuine Articulation

Peaceful Correspondence urges us to genuinely articulate our thoughts. Valid articulation implies being consistent with ourselves and sharing our contemplations, feelings, needs, and wants genuinely and powerlessly. It includes utilizing "I" proclamations to get a sense of ownership with our own encounters and keeping away from fault or analysis. By imparting really, we welcome others to do likewise, sustaining further associations and trust.

Peaceful Language

Peaceful Correspondence puts incredible significance on utilizing peaceful language. Peaceful language is described by clearness, regard, and an emphasis on perceptions instead of assessments. It dodges language that is critical, accusatory, or coercive. By expressing ourselves carefully and communicating in peaceful language, we can lessen protectiveness, limit clashes, and encourage more agreeable connections.

Developing Ability to Understand Individuals On a Deeper Level

The capacity to appreciate anyone on a deeper level is the capacity to perceive, comprehend, and deal with our own feelings, as well as the feelings of others. Peaceful Correspondence assists us with creating the capacity to understand people on a deeper level by empowering us to interface with and express our sentiments in a productive manner. By developing the capacity to understand people on a deeper level, we upgrade our capacity to identify, successfully, and fabricate solid and sound connections.

Nonverbal Correspondence

While language envelops verbal correspondence, nonverbal correspondence likewise assumes a huge part in our connections. Nonverbal signals like non-verbal communication, looks, motions, and manner of speaking can convey importance and feelings that words alone may not catch. Peaceful Correspondence underlines the significance of focusing on nonverbal signals, as they frequently give extra bits of knowledge into the speaker's sentiments and requirements.

Regarding Contrasts

In connections, it is unavoidable that people will have alternate points of view, values, and needs. Peaceful Correspondence trains us to regard and respect these distinctions. It urges us to tune in with a receptive outlook, look for understanding, and settle on something worth agreeing on in any event, when our perspectives might veer. By regarding contrasts and moving toward clashes with sympathy and interest, we can connect partitions and encourage understanding.

Building Trust and Association

Powerful correspondence is a vital driver of trust and association in connections. Peaceful Correspondence gives apparatuses and procedures to fabricate trust and association. By utilizing language that tells the truth, conscious, and merciful, we establish a climate that supports receptiveness and weakness. Through empathic tuning in, genuine articulation, and peaceful language, we can lay out and fortify bonds with others.

Language is an amazing asset that shapes our connections. By integrating the standards of Peaceful Correspondence into our language and correspondence rehearses, we can change our connections. Careful correspondence, empathic tuning in, legitimate articulation, peaceful language, developing capacity to appreciate people on a deeper level, taking care of nonverbal signs, regarding contrasts, and building trust and association are necessary parts of utilizing language successfully in connections. In the accompanying parts, we will dig further into explicit correspondence methods and systems presented by Peaceful Correspondence to improve our language abilities and make considerably additional satisfying connections.

CHANGING CLASH WITH PEACEFULNESS

Struggle is a characteristic and unavoidable piece of human connection. Whether it emerges in private, proficient, or cultural settings, clashes can be wellsprings of strain, misjudging, and even brutality. Notwithstanding, it is possible to change clashes into open doors for development, understanding, and association through the act of peacefulness. In this section, we will investigate how Peaceful Correspondence (PC) and other peaceful methodologies can assist us with exploring clashes calmly and cultivate positive results.

Understanding Conflict

To transform conflict, it is essential to first understand its nature. Conflict arises when there is a clash of interests, needs, or values between individuals or groups. It can manifest as disagreements, power struggles, or even deep-rooted societal divisions. peaceful correspondence recognizes conflicts as opportunities for dialogue, learning, and growth. Instead of avoiding or escalating conflicts, PC offers a framework for transforming them into constructive interactions.

Peaceful correspondence and Conflict Resolution

peaceful correspondence provides a powerful approach to conflict resolution by emphasizing empathy, understanding, and collaboration. It offers practical tools for expressing ourselves authentically, listening empathically, and finding win-win solutions. By practicing PC, individuals can engage in respectful dialogue, identify shared needs, and seek resolutions that address the underlying concerns of all parties involved.

Empathy in Conflict Resolution

Empathy is a key element in transforming conflict with nonviolence. It involves actively listening to the perspectives, feelings, and needs of all parties involved without judgment or blame. Empathy creates a safe space for individuals to be heard and understood, fostering mutual respect and connection. By cultivating empathy, we can bridge divides, find common ground, and work collaboratively toward resolution.

Active Listening and Reflection

Active listening is an essential skill in conflict resolution. It requires giving our full attention, maintaining eye contact, and being fully present with the speaker. Active listening also involves reflecting back what we have heard to ensure accurate understanding and demonstrate our genuine interest in the other person's experience. By engaging in active listening, we create an atmosphere of openness and receptivity that can contribute to effective conflict transformation.

Managing Emotions

Conflicts can trigger strong emotions, such as anger, frustration, or fear. peaceful correspondence encourages individuals to recognize and manage their emotions in conflict situations. By taking responsibility for our own emotional responses and developing emotional intelligence, we can respond to conflicts with calmness and clarity. Emotional regulation enables us to approach conflicts nonviolently and maintain a focus on understanding and resolution.

Mediation and Facilitation

In more complex or intense conflicts, the involvement of a neutral third party can be beneficial. Mediation and facilitation techniques informed by peaceful correspondence principles can guide conflicting parties toward resolution. Mediators or facilitators create a safe and structured environment, allowing individuals to express their needs, concerns, and perspectives while fostering understanding and collaboration. Through the mediation process, conflicting parties can work together to find mutually acceptable solutions.

Nonviolence as a Path to Healing

Conflict can leave emotional wounds and strain relationships. Nonviolence provides a path to healing by fostering forgiveness, understanding, and reconciliation. By embracing nonviolence, individuals can let go of resentment, acknowledge the impact of the conflict, and work towards rebuilding trust and repairing damaged relationships. Nonviolence promotes a sense of shared humanity and interconnectedness, allowing conflicts to be transformed into opportunities for personal and collective growth.

Peaceful Activism and Societal Transformation

Nonviolence is not limited to personal conflicts; it can also be a powerful force for social and systemic change. Peaceful activism rooted in nonviolence has a long history of inspiring social movements and challenging oppressive systems. By utilizing nonviolent strategies such as civil disobedience, grassroots organizing, and constructive dialogue, individuals and communities can address structural conflicts and work towards creating a more just and equitable society.

Conflict can be transformed into a catalyst for growth, understanding, and connection through the practice of nonviolence. Peaceful correspondence offers practical tools for conflict resolution, such as empathy, active listening, emotional regulation, mediation, and facilitation. By embracing nonviolence as a personal and societal approach, conflicts can become opportunities for learning, reconciliation, and positive change. In the following chapters, we will explore further techniques and examples of nonviolent conflict resolution, providing readers with the knowledge and skills to navigate conflicts nonviolently and contribute to a more peaceful world.

CHAPTER 2:

Noticing, Feeling, And Requiring

In Peaceful correspondence (PC), the course of compelling correspondence starts with noticing, feeling, and requiring. These three parts structure the underpinning of figuring out ourselves as well as other people on a more profound level. In this part, we will investigate the significance of perception, the job of sentiments in correspondence, and the basic necessities that drive our ways of behaving. By creating mindfulness and understanding around there, we can upgrade our capacity to associate, relate, and impart truly.

The Force of Perception

Perception is the act of depicting what we see without assessment, judgment, or understanding. It includes zeroing in on current realities and ways of behaving that we can straightforwardly see, as opposed to making presumptions or crediting thought processes to other people. Perceptions give a strong ground to successful correspondence since they welcome lucidity, decrease misconceptions, and consider mutual perspective. By developing the expertise of genuine perception, we can construct areas of strength for empathic and peaceful correspondence.

The Job of Sentiments

Sentiments are a necessary piece of the human experience. They furnish us with important data about our internal state and the effect of our encounters. quiet correspondence underscores the significance of interfacing with and communicating our sentiments sincerely and really. By monitoring our own sentiments and perceiving the sensations of others, we can extend our figuring out, cultivate sympathy, and establish a climate helpful for open discourse and association.

Distinguishing Needs

At the center of our feelings and ways of behaving lie our necessities. Needs address the general, basic human necessities that drive our activities. quiet correspondence urges us to distinguish and communicate our requirements obviously and straightforwardly. By recognizing and regarding our own requirements, as well as perceiving the necessities of others, we can develop grasping, empathy, and joint effort. Needs-engaged correspondence encourages a feeling of shared humankind and supports the production of arrangements that address everybody's issues.

The Interchange of Perceptions, Sentiments, and Requirements

Perceptions, sentiments, and necessities are interconnected and impact each other in correspondence. Our perceptions trigger our sentiments, which thus mirror our basic requirements. By focusing on our perceptions and the sentiments they bring out, we gain bits of knowledge into our requirements and the necessities of others. tranquil correspondence urges us to investigate this interchange intentionally, considering a more profound comprehension of ourselves and encouraging compassion and association with people around us.

Sympathy and Understanding

Noticing, feeling, and requiring are fundamental parts of compassion and understanding. Sympathy includes effectively tuning in, recognizing and approving the sentiments and necessities of others. peaceful correspondence trains us to listen empathically, suspending judgment and trying to grasp the encounters of others. By checking out their perceptions, sentiments, and requirements, we can foster a significant feeling of association and establish a climate where everybody feels appreciated and comprehended.

Respecting and Communicating Sentiments

peaceful correspondence urges us to truly respect and express our sentiments. By creating profound proficiency and becoming mindful of our close to home scene, we can explain our sentiments with lucidity and accuracy. At the point when we express our sentiments genuinely and helplessly, we welcome others to identify with us and extend how they might interpret our encounters. Respecting and communicating our sentiments is a vital part of creating certifiable associations and settling clashes calmly.

Needs as a Main thrust

Perceiving and tending to needs is indispensable for successful correspondence and compromise. Our necessities shape our ways of behaving, inspirations, and connections. quiet correspondence underlines the significance of distinguishing and communicating needs in a manner that is clear, explicit, and liberated from requests or pressure. By zeroing in on needs as opposed to on fixed positions or techniques, we open up opportunities for cooperative arrangements and cultivate common comprehension and regard.

Engaging Arrangements

Noticing, feeling, and requiring engage us to find valuable arrangements that address the issues of all gatherings included. quiet correspondence supports a shift from issue centered thinking to a requirements centered approach. By investigating shared needs and looking for commonly gainful results, we can participate in imaginative critical thinking and create mutual benefit arrangements. This approach cultivates joint effort, sympathy, and long haul agreement in our connections.

Rehearsing Self-Sympathy

Noticing, feeling, and requiring additionally apply to our relationship with ourselves. peaceful correspondence welcomes us to develop self-sympathy by noticing our inward encounters, recognizing our sentiments, and perceiving our requirements. By creating mindfulness and stretching out compassion and understanding to ourselves, we can upgrade our general prosperity and work on our ability for legitimate correspondence with others.

Noticing, feeling, and requiring are crucial parts of Peaceful Correspondence. By developing the expertise of genuine perception, interfacing with our sentiments legitimately, and perceiving the fundamental necessities that drive our ways of behaving, we lay the foundation for empathic and peaceful correspondence. Through this interaction, we extend how we might interpret ourselves as well as other people, cultivate sympathy and association, and make an additional agreeable and sympathetic world. In the accompanying sections, we will dive further into explicit procedures and techniques presented by tranquil correspondence to upgrade our capacity to notice, feel, and interface on a more profound level.

CREATING MINDFULNESS

Creating mindfulness is a fundamental part of peaceful correspondence (PC) that permits us to take part in viable and humane correspondence. In this part, we will investigate the significance of creating mindfulness, the job of care in developing mindfulness, and useful techniques to upgrade our mindfulness and comprehension of others. By creating mindfulness, we can extend our association, encourage compassion, and make amicable connections.

The Meaning of Creating Mindfulness

Creating mindfulness is a fundamental part of PC. It includes developing a profound comprehension of ourselves, others, and the elements of correspondence. Mindfulness permits us to perceive our own examples, triggers, and needs, as well as those of others. It empowers us to move toward clashes and difficulties with sympathy and empathy, cultivating understanding and collaboration. Creating mindfulness is a persistent cycle that improves our relational abilities and adds to self-improvement and change.

The Act of Care

Care is a useful asset for creating mindfulness. It includes giving intentional consideration to the current second with a nonjudgmental and tolerating mentality. Care assists us with noticing our contemplations, sentiments, substantial sensations, and the general climate without connection or reactivity. By rehearsing care, we develop a condition of uplifted mindfulness that empowers us to answer deliberately, as opposed to responsively, in our correspondence and communications.

Developing Mindfulness

Mindfulness is a critical part of creating mindfulness. It includes developing comprehension: we might interpret our own considerations, feelings, convictions, and ways of behaving. Mindfulness permits us to perceive our triggers, designs, and neglected needs. Through self-reflection, self-request, and practices like journaling or contemplation, we can investigate our inward scene and gain experiences into our inspirations, values, and yearnings. Developing mindfulness enables us to impart really and settle on cognizant decisions lined up with our qualities.

Creating Compassion

Compassion is a central part of PC and requires a profound familiarity with others' encounters and points of view. Creating compassion includes listening mindfully, suspending judgment, and trying to grasp others' sentiments and requirements. By developing compassion, we associate on a more profound level, recognize the humankind in others, and make a place of refuge for open and legitimate correspondence. Sympathy upgrades our capacity to calmly answer sympathetically and resolve clashes.

Peaceful Self-Talk

Creating mindfulness likewise stretches out to our interior discourse and self-talk. Peaceful self-talk includes noticing and changing our internal analysis, decisions, and self-fault into sympathetic and steady contemplations. By developing self-sympathy and addressing ourselves with thoughtfulness and understanding, we foster a better relationship with ourselves. Peaceful self-talk adds to mindfulness, self-acknowledgement, and a more noteworthy limit with respect to sympathy towards others.

Noticing Contemplations and Feelings

Creating mindfulness expects us to notice our contemplations and feelings without getting snared in them. By becoming mindful of our thinking designs and close to home responses, we can acquire understanding into the basic requirements and values that drive our way of behaving. Through careful perception, we withdraw from our viewpoints and feelings, permitting us to answer more deliberately as opposed to being driven by oblivious examples or programmed responses.

Intelligent Tuning in

Intelligent listening is a training that upgrades our familiarity with others' encounters. It includes rewording or summing up what somebody has said to guarantee exact comprehension. Intelligent listening shows that we are completely present and participated in the discussion, empowering the speaker to share all the more profoundly. By effectively tuning in and reflecting back what we hear, we develop a more profound familiarity with others' viewpoints and cultivate sympathy and association.

Looking for Input

Creating mindfulness includes being available to getting input from others. Looking for input gives important experiences into what our words and activities mean for other people. By welcoming legitimate and valuable criticism, we develop how we might interpret how our correspondence is seen and can make changes as needs be. Looking for criticism likewise shows an eagerness to learn and develop, encouraging trust and cooperation in our connections.

Rehearsing Nonjudgmental Perception

Nonjudgmental perception is a center practice in PC. It includes depicting perceptions without assessing, condemning, or crediting thought processes. By developing nonjudgmental perception, we cultivate clearness, decrease protectiveness, and make a place of refuge for open discourse. Nonjudgmental perception permits us to zero in on realities as opposed to presumptions or translations, improving our mindfulness and comprehension of ourselves as well as other people.

Creating mindfulness is an extraordinary practice that empowers us to take part in merciful and compelling correspondence. By developing care, mindfulness, compassion, and nonjudgmental perception, we extend how we might interpret ourselves as well as other people. Creating mindfulness engages us to convey truly, explore clashes calmly, and fabricate agreeable connections. In the accompanying sections, we will dive further into explicit procedures and methodologies presented by PC to further foster our mindfulness and improve our relational abilities.

NOTICING VERSUS ASSESSING

In peaceful correspondence (PC), the qualification among noticing and assessing is a pivotal part of powerful correspondence and compromise. Noticing includes portraying objective realities and ways of behaving without judgment or translation, while assessing includes making decisions, correlations, or crediting intentions to others' activities. In this section, we will investigate the meaning of noticing as opposed to assessing, the effect of assessment on correspondence, and reasonable systems to upgrade our capacity to notice nonjudgmentally to cultivate understanding and association.

The Significance of Noticing versus Assessing

Noticing and assessing are two particular approaches to seeing and figuring out our general surroundings. Fostering the ability of nonjudgmental perception is fundamental for viable correspondence and compromise. At the point when we see without assessment, we make a space for clearness, understanding, and association. By perceiving the distinction among noticing and assessing, we can change critical correspondence designs and develop sympathy and empathy in our communications.

Grasping Nonjudgmental Perception

Nonjudgmental perception includes portraying what we straightforwardly notice, without forcing our decisions, translations, or individual predispositions. It centers around genuine realities, ways of behaving, and tangible data that can be checked by others. Nonjudgmental perception considers common perspective and decreases the potential for protectiveness or misconception. By fostering the ability to notice nonjudgmentally, we make an establishment for viable correspondence and compromise.

Understanding the effect of assessment on correspondence

Assessment in correspondence frequently prompts separation, struggle, and incapable critical thinking. At the point when we assess, we force our emotional suppositions, suspicions, and understandings onto others' ways of behaving or words. This can set off protectiveness, opposition, and the breakdown of compassion. Assessment frequently conveys a feeling of judgment, fault, or analysis, upsetting open exchange and understanding. Understanding the effect of assessment on correspondence rouses us to move towards nonjudgmental perception.

Developing Nonjudgmental Perception

Developing the act of nonjudgmental perception requires care and mindfulness. It includes deliberately seeing our propensity to assess and deciding to suspend judgment. By fostering the capacity to isolate perceptions from assessments, we can make a space for more profound comprehension and compassion. Developing nonjudgmental perception is a persistent cycle that includes self-reflection, purposefulness, and a promise to merciful correspondence.

Utilizing Objective Language

Objective language is a fundamental part of nonjudgmental perception. It includes utilizing clear and explicit language that depicts detectable realities, ways of behaving, or occasions. By zeroing in on what can be straightforwardly seen or heard, we lessen the probability of errors and protectiveness. Objective language permits us to impart such things that welcome understanding and participation, improving our capacity to interface with others.

Addressing Suppositions

Creating nonjudgmental perception requires interrogating the suppositions we hold regarding others. Suppositions can cloud our discernments and lead to one-sided translations. By developing interest and a readiness to challenge our suspicions, we open ourselves to a more extensive viewpoint and more prominent comprehension. Addressing presumptions permits us to move toward correspondence with transparency, sympathy, and a certifiable longing to gain from others.

Intelligent Tuning in

Intelligent listening is a strong strategy that upholds nonjudgmental perception. It includes rewording or summing up what the speaker has said to show precise comprehension. Intelligent listening permits the speaker to feel appreciated and recognized, cultivating trust and transparency. By rehearsing intelligent tuning in, we take part in nonjudgmental perception and establish a climate that energizes legitimate and significant discourse.

Developing Sympathy

Nonjudgmental perception is firmly interwoven with sympathy. Compassion includes understanding and discussing the thoughts and points of view of others. By suspending judgment and noticing nonjudgmentally, we make space for compassion to arise. Developing compassion permits us to interface profoundly with others, appreciate their encounters, and convey such things that praise their necessities and values.

Changing Evaluative Language

Changing evaluative language into nonjudgmental perception is a strong method for improving correspondence. It expects us to focus on our language decisions, supplant evaluative explanations with true portrayals, and spotlight on unambiguous ways of behaving instead of making speculations. By intentionally changing evaluative language, we make an environment of regard, understanding, and coordinated effort, encouraging successful correspondence and compromise.

Noticing as opposed to assessing is a critical differentiation in Peaceful Correspondence. By fostering the expertise of nonjudgmental perception, we make an establishment for viable correspondence, understanding, and association. Developing nonjudgmental perception includes care, addressing suppositions, utilizing objective language, and rehearsing intelligent tuning in. Through nonjudgmental perception, we welcome sympathy, empathy, and powerful compromise into our communications. In the accompanying parts, we will dive further into explicit procedures and methodologies presented by tranquil correspondence to upgrade our capacity to notice nonjudgmentally and speak with genuineness and compassion.

COMMUNICATING SENTIMENTS AND DISTINGUISHING NEEDS

In Peaceful correspondence (PC), the statement of sentiments and the ID of necessities assume a crucial part in making bona fide and sympathetic correspondence. Understanding and really communicating our sentiments, as well as distinguishing the hidden necessities behind those sentiments, permit us to interface with ourselves as well as other people on a more profound level. In this section, we will investigate the significance of communicating sentiments and recognizing needs, commonsense systems for doing as such, and the extraordinary force of this cycle in upgrading our connections and encouraging comprehension.

The Meaning of Communicating Sentiments

Communicating sentiments is a fundamental part of compelling correspondence. Sentiments give important data about our inward encounters, needs, and the effect of outer occasions on our prosperity. At the point when we express our sentiments genuinely and really, we welcome others to comprehend and interface with us at a more profound level. The capacity to communicate our sentiments straightforwardly takes into consideration certifiable association, sympathy, and the structure of agreeable connections.

Developing Close to home Education

Close to home proficiency is the capacity to perceive, comprehend, and express our feelings precisely. It includes creating familiarity with the various feelings we experience and having the option to successfully name and lucid them. By developing close to home education, we become more on top of our sentiments and better prepared to communicate them in an unmistakable and valuable way. Close to home proficiency upholds mindfulness and enables us to explore our profound scene with empathy and genuineness.

Making a Place of refuge for Close to home Articulation

Making a place of refuge for close to home articulation is fundamental for encouraging transparent correspondence. At the point when we establish a climate liberated from judgment, analysis, and refutation, we welcome others to talk about their thoughts unafraid of dismissal. Undivided attention, sympathy, and nonjudgmental acknowledgment add to the making of a place of refuge, permitting people to communicate their feelings truly and encouraging further comprehension and association.

Viable Techniques for Communicating Sentiments

Communicating sentiments successfully includes utilizing "I" articulations, possessing our feelings, and being explicit in our correspondence. By utilizing "I" articulations, we assume a sense of ownership with our sentiments and try not to fault or charge others. Claiming our feelings permits us to communicate them without anticipating that others should "fix" or change them. Being explicit in our correspondence gives lucidity and helps other people comprehend the particular sentiments we are encountering. These techniques support true articulation and advance productive exchange.

The Job of Undivided attention

Undivided attention is a fundamental part of making a space for communicating sentiments. At the point when we participate in undivided attention, we concentrate on the speaker, show compassion, and approve their sentiments. Undivided attention includes being available, keeping in touch, and giving verbal and nonverbal signals to demonstrate that we are completely taken part in the discussion. By rehearsing undivided attention, we establish a strong climate for the outflow of sentiments and cultivate further comprehension and association.

The Connection Among Sentiments and Necessities

Sentiments are firmly connected to our hidden necessities. Distinguishing and understanding the necessities behind our sentiments is an urgent move toward compelling correspondence. Needs address our crucial human prerequisites that drive our ways of behaving and shape our co operations. By perceiving and communicating our requirements, we welcome comprehension and joint effort. Understanding the association between our sentiments and necessities empowers us to convey such that cultivates sympathy, shared regard, and innovative critical thinking.

47

Procedures for Recognizing Needs

Distinguishing needs includes creating mindfulness, rehearsing reflection, and focusing on the fundamental inspirations driving our sentiments. Journaling, self-reflection, and care procedures can uphold the method involved with recognizing needs. By investigating the more profound layers of our feelings.

CHAPTER 3:

Making Caring Solicitations

Making sympathetic solicitations is a critical part of peaceful correspondence (PC) that permits us to communicate our requirements and wants while encouraging comprehension and association. In this section, we will investigate the significance of making empathetic solicitations, the standards behind successful solicitations, and functional systems to form demands that advance joint effort and collaboration. By excelling at making empathetic solicitations, we can establish a climate of sympathy, regard, and common fulfillment.

The Meaning of Making Empathetic Solicitations

Making caring solicitations is fundamental for viable correspondence and compromise. By obviously and self-assuredly communicating our necessities, we set out open doors for understanding and joint effort. Sympathetic solicitations permit us to explore clashes, arrange arrangements, and assemble agreeable connections. They work with open exchange, advance shared regard, and add to the formation of mutual benefit results.

The Standards of Powerful Demands

Powerful demands are grounded in specific rules that help positive correspondence. They are explicit, positive, practical, and arranged toward activity. Viable solicitations center around what we need instead of what we don't need, which engages the two players to pursue a common objective. By getting it and applying these standards, we can improve the probability of our solicitations being heard, comprehended, and met with eagerness.

Building Sympathy and Association

Humane solicitations are not requests or ultimatums but rather solicitations to understand team up. They cultivate sympathy by featuring our fundamental necessities and communicating our weakness. By setting demands as opposed to expectations, we make a space for understanding and association. Empathetic solicitations show our regard for the independence and prosperity of others, sustaining trust and cultivating a feeling of participation.

Forming Clear and Brief Solicitations

Planning clear and compact solicitations is significant for compelling correspondence. Clearness guarantees that our solicitations are handily figured out, ruling out confusion. Compactness tries not to overpower the audience with unreasonable subtleties or pointless data. By finding an opportunity to explain our solicitations, we improve the probability of them being gotten and tended to actually.

Utilizing Positive and Explicit Language

Positive and explicit language upgrades the viability of solicitations. Positive language centers around what we need, as opposed to what we don't need, advancing a useful and arrangement situated approach. Explicit language gives clear direction and diminishes equivocalness. By utilizing positive and explicit language, we increment the clearness and effect of our solicitations, working with understanding and participation.

Undivided attention Because of Solicitations

Undivided attention is a basic part of answering solicitations humanely. It includes really focusing, showing compassion, and looking to figure out the necessities and goals behind the solicitation. By participating in undivided attention, we establish a climate that empowers open exchange and joint effort. Undivided attention permits us to answer with compassion and track down commonly fulfilling arrangements.

Arranging and Working together

Empathetic solicitations welcome discussion and joint effort. They perceive the necessities and points of view of the two players included, trying to find mutual benefit arrangements. Arranging and teaming up require liberality, adaptability, and an eagerness to investigate choices. By embracing a cooperative mentality, we can cultivate understanding, form trust, and make results that address the issues of all included.

Demands in Various Settings

Making sympathetic solicitations applies to different settings, including individual connections, workplaces, and local area settings. The standards and techniques for causing solicitations to stay reliable across settings. Be that as it may, the particular elements and contemplations might shift. By understanding how to adjust our solicitations to various settings, we can explore assorted circumstances and encourage positive and productive correspondence.

Coordinating Caring Solicitations in Day to day existence

Making merciful solicitations is an expertise that can be incorporated into our regular routines. By integrating the standards and procedures of Peaceful Correspondence, we improve our capacity to communicate our necessities actually and assemble amicable connections. Reliable practice permits us to develop a correspondence style that is grounded in sympathy, regard, and participation.

Making caring solicitations is an amazing asset for successful correspondence and compromise. By grasping the standards of powerful demands, utilizing positive and explicit language, and embracing exchange and cooperation, we cultivate figuring out, compassion, and association. Humane solicitations establish a climate that empowers open discourse, shared regard, and the quest for mutual benefit arrangements. In the accompanying parts, we will dive further into explicit methods and systems presented by quiet correspondence to further upgrade our capacity to make humane solicitations, advancing positive and amicable connections in all aspects of our lives.

FORMING VIABLE SOLICITATIONS

Forming viable solicitations is a fundamental ability in Peaceful correspondence (PC) that permits us to impart our requirements and wants obviously and decisively. In this section, we will investigate the meaning of forming powerful demands, the parts of a very much created demand, and commonsense techniques to guarantee our solicitations are received and perceived. By excelling at forming powerful demands, we can improve the probability of our necessities being met and make an establishment for amicable and cooperative correspondence.

The Significance of Forming Successful Solicitations

Figuring out powerful demands is urgent for accomplishing lucidity, understanding, and participation in correspondence. Demands give a reasonable heading to others to address our issues, and they can act as impetus for coordinated effort and critical thinking. By planning demands actually, we enable ourselves as well as other people to participate in open exchange, investigate conceivable outcomes, and track down commonly fulfilling arrangements.

The Parts of a Compelling Solicitation

Compelling solicitations comprise of a few key parts that add to their clearness and effect. These parts incorporate a particular activity, an unmistakable time span, and a positive concentration. By integrating these components, we guarantee that our solicitations are exact, significant, and zeroed in on what we need to accomplish. This clearness upgrades the possibilities of our solicitations being perceived and tended to really.

Making a Positive Casing

Outlining demands in a positive way is a strong methodology for powerful correspondence. Positive outlining centers around what we want or need, as opposed to what we need or need to stay away from. By communicating our solicitations emphatically, we make an air of cooperation, hopefulness, and probability. Positive outlining welcomes innovativeness, empowers commitment, and supports the advancement of arrangements that address everybody's issues.

Taking into account Attainability

Planning viable solicitations includes thinking about the practicality of our solicitations. Plausibility alludes to the reasonableness and probability of satisfying the solicitation. By surveying the assets, limitations, and conditions included, we can tailor our solicitations to line up with what is reasonably feasible. Taking into account practicality upgrades the possibilities of our solicitations being met and cultivates a feeling of trust and unwavering quality in our correspondence.

Undivided attention and Explanation

Figuring out successful solicitations requires undivided attention and explanation. Undivided attention includes mindfulness and sympathetic attention to the necessities and viewpoints of others. Explanation includes looking for understanding by getting clarification on some things, summing up, and reflecting back what has been said. By taking part in undivided attention and explanation, we guarantee that our solicitations depend on exact comprehension, advancing compelling correspondence and cooperation.

Adjusting Decisiveness and Adaptability

Figuring out powerful demands requires a harmony among emphaticness and adaptability. Confidence permits us to communicate our requirements and limits without animosity or antagonism obviously. Adaptability includes being available to elective arrangements and taking into account the requirements of others. By finding some kind of harmony among emphaticness and adaptability, we establish a climate that empowers discourse, understanding, and the investigation of inventive conceivable outcomes.

Amending and Refining Solicitations

Forming viable solicitations is an iterative cycle that might require updates and refinements. As we take part in open discourse and get criticism, we might find new data or points of view that require changes in accordance with our underlying solicitations. By being available to modify and refine our solicitations, we show a readiness to team up, adjust, and find arrangements that meet the developing requirements of all gatherings included.

Explaining Assumptions and Arrangements

Planning viable solicitations includes explaining assumptions and arrangements. This incorporates examining and arriving at a common perspective of what will be finished, by whom, and inside what time period. Explaining assumptions and arrangements forestalls false impressions, guarantees responsibility, and cultivates a feeling of trust and unwavering quality in our correspondence. It likewise gives an establishment to assessing progress and tending to any potential difficulties that might emerge.

Rehearsing Sympathy and Understanding

Figuring out successful solicitations isn't exclusively centered around our own necessities; it additionally includes thinking about the requirements and viewpoints of others. By rehearsing sympathy and understanding, we can tailor our solicitations such that regards

POSITIVE AND EXPLICIT LANGUAGE

Utilizing positive and explicit language is a strong part of quiet correspondence (PC) that upholds successful correspondence, understanding, and association. In this part, we will investigate the significance of positive and explicit language, what it means for our corporations, and functional systems to integrate positive and explicit language into our correspondence. By dominating the utilization of positive and explicit language, we can upgrade our capacity to communicate our thoughts really, construct agreeable connections, and make a positive effect in our corporations.

The Meaning of Positive and Explicit Language

Positive and explicit language shapes our correspondence and the manner in which others see us.

It can impact the general tone of a discussion, set a valuable and cooperative climate, and work with understanding. By utilizing positive and explicit language, we make space for sympathy, association, and the shared fulfillment of requirements. It considers clearness, diminishes misconceptions, and encourages a feeling of regard and collaboration.

Moving from Negative to Positive Language

Moving from negative to positive language includes rethinking our correspondence to zero in on what we need, as opposed to what we don't need. Negative language frequently accentuates fault, analysis, or what is deficient with regards to, which can make protectiveness and block compelling correspondence. By deliberately picking positive language, we rouse joint effort, empower inventive critical thinking, and develop a hopeful and useful environment.

Distinguishing and Communicating Wants

Positive language includes distinguishing and communicating our longings and yearnings. It permits us to explain what we need to accomplish, insight, or make. By communicating our longings decidedly, we welcome others to participate in a cooperative investigation of conceivable outcomes. Distinguishing and communicating wants assists us with imparting our qualities, interests, and objectives, encouraging comprehension and association with others.

Involving Explicit Language for Clearness

Explicit language is instrumental in passing on clear and exact messages. It gives subtleties, models, and substantial data that dispense with uncertainty and disarray. By utilizing explicit language, we guarantee that our correspondence is handily perceived and pretty much rules out error. Explicit language upholds undivided attention, sympathy, and precise appreciation of our expectations and necessities.

Zeroing in on Perceptions and Realities

Positive and explicit language frequently spins around perceptions and realities as opposed to suppositions or understandings. By depicting discernible ways of behaving or occasions, we anchor our correspondence in true reality. Zeroing in on perceptions and realities upholds nonjudgmental correspondence, diminishes protectiveness, and advances common perspective. By featuring explicit ways of behaving, we stay away from speculations and welcome valuable exchange.

Outlining Solicitations in Certain Language

Positive language is particularly significant while figuring out demands. By outlining our solicitations emphatically, we center around what we need to witness, instead of what we don't need. Positive outlining works with coordinated effort, spurs others to contribute, and improves the probability of our solicitations being gotten with transparency. By articulating our solicitations in certain languages, we create a climate of probability and mutual perspective.

Rehearsing Self-Talk with Positive Language

Positive language stretches out to our inward exchange and self-talk. By utilizing positive language while addressing ourselves, we develop self-sympathy, self-acknowledgement, and flexibility. Positive self-talk empowers a mentality of development, cultivates fearlessness, and supports our general prosperity. By deliberately picking positive language in our self-talk, we support a positive mental self portrait and improve our correspondence with others.

Offering Appreciation and Thanks

Positive language incorporates offering appreciation and thanks. By recognizing and offering thanks for the activities, characteristics, or endeavors of others, we reinforce our associations and advance a positive and steady environment. Appreciation and appreciation build up certain correspondence designs, approve the commitments of others, and cultivate a feeling of having a place and appreciation in our connections.

Coordinating Positive and Explicit Language in Day to day existence

Utilizing positive and explicit language is a training that can be coordinated into our regular routines. By being aware of our language decisions, rethinking negative explanations into positive ones, and being explicit in our correspondence, we upgrade the lucidity, adequacy, and positive effect of our collaborations. Reliably integrating positive and explicit language into our correspondence encourages sympathy, understanding, and participation, prompting more agreeable and satisfying connections.

Utilizing positive and explicit language is an extraordinary part of Peaceful Correspondence. By moving from negative to positive language, recognizing and communicating wants, involving explicit language for clearness, and zeroing in on perceptions and realities, we improve our capacity to convey truly and productively. Outlining demands in sure language, rehearsing self-talk with positive language, and offering appreciation and thanks further add to positive and amicable correspondence. By incorporating positive and explicit language into our day to day routines, we develop a climate of sympathy, regard, and coordinated effort. In the accompanying parts, we will dive further into explicit methods and techniques presented by quiet correspondence to improve our utilization of positive and explicit language, working with significant and humane correspondence in all aspects of our lives.

DEMANDS IN CONNECTIONS

Demands assume an essential part in cultivating sound and agreeable connections. In this section, we will investigate the meaning of solicitations in connections, the difficulties that might emerge, and pragmatic methodologies for causing demands that to advance getting it, association, and common fulfillment. By excelling at making demands in connections, we can explore clashes, fortify close to home bonds, and develop a common feeling of congruity and development.

The Significance of Solicitations in Connections

Demands act as an establishment for compelling correspondence and critical thinking in connections. They give a road to communicating our necessities, wants, and limits, as well as a method for haggling commonly fulfilling arrangements. By making demands, we engage ourselves and our accomplices to participate in the co-formation of a satisfying and agreeable relationship effectively.

Exploring Power Elements

Demands in connections can be affected by power elements. It is vital to perceive and address any uneven characters that might exist. By advancing open discourse, undivided attention, and equivalent cooperation, we establish a climate that empowers the statement of necessities and wants from all gatherings included. Exploring power elements with awareness and compassion takes into consideration deferential and cooperative correspondence.

Developing Sympathy and Understanding

Making demands in connections requires developing sympathy and understanding. By taking into account the requirements and viewpoints of our accomplices, we make a space for shared understanding and association. Sympathy permits us to move toward demands with empathy and to think about the effect of our activities on others. Understanding the fundamental necessities and upsides of our accomplices assists us with forming demands that impact them and add to a common feeling of prosperity.

Undivided attention and Approval

Undivided attention and approval are fundamental parts of making demands in connections. At the point when we listen mindfully and approve our accomplices' sentiments and requirements, we make a protected and steady space for open correspondence. By effectively tuning in, we exhibit regard and certifiable interest in grasping our accomplices' viewpoints. Approval cultivates trust, sympathy, and the ability to address each other's issues.

Respecting Individual Independence and Limits

Making demands in connections includes respecting the independence and limits of the two accomplices. Perceiving and regarding individual independence implies recognizing that every individual has the privilege to simply decide and choices that line up with their qualities and necessities. By being aware of limits and looking for assent, we establish a climate of trust, security, and regard in which solicitations can be made and haggled with responsiveness and thought.

Joint effort and Exchange

Demands in connections frequently require joint effort and exchange. By participating in open discourse, conceptualizing arrangements, and looking for commonly fulfilling results, we advance shared liability and the co-production of an amicable relationship.

Cooperation and exchange include dynamic interest, adaptability, and an eagerness to find shared benefit arrangements that honor the requirements and upsides of the two accomplices.

Adjusting Individual and Relationship Needs

Offsetting individual requirements with the necessities of the relationship is a fragile part of making demands. It requires progressing correspondence, split the difference, and a promise to the development and prosperity of the two people and the actual relationship. By perceiving that singular requirements add to the general soundness of the relationship, we make an establishment for grasping, sympathy, and common help.

Thinking about Criticism and Changing Solicitations

Demands in connections might require reflection, criticism, and changes. It means quite a bit to be available to get criticism from our accomplices and to ponder what our solicitations mean for them. By integrating criticism and changing our solicitations likewise, we show a readiness to develop and learn.

PART II
PEACEFUL CORRESPONDENCE IN RELATIONSHIPS

CHAPTER 4:

Sustaining Trust And Closeness

Supporting trust and closeness is a foundation of solid and satisfying connections. In this section, we will investigate the significance of trust and closeness, the variables that add to their turn of events and support, and pragmatic systems for sustaining trust and developing profound association. By understanding the elements of trust and closeness, we can make connections that are grounded in validness, weakness, and common regard.

The Meaning of Trust and Closeness

Trust and closeness are fundamental for building solid and versatile connections. Trust makes a feeling that everything is safe and secure, dependable, and trust in each other. Closeness includes profound closeness, weakness, and a readiness to be seen and perceived. Trust and closeness make an establishment for open correspondence, shared help, and the investigation of more profound degrees of association.

Figuring out Trust

Trust is worked over the long run through steady activities, unwavering quality, and straightforwardness. It includes putting stock in the dependability and generosity of our accomplices. Trust is supported by regarding responsibilities, telling the truth and straightforwardly, and showing respectability in our activities. Trust permits us to have a good sense of reassurance, acknowledged, and esteemed in our connections, cultivating a feeling of close to home wellbeing and opportunity.

Developing Weakness

Weakness is a vital fixing in extending close to home association and supporting trust. It includes the ability to be open, legitimate, and bona fide with our accomplices. By embracing weakness, we establish a climate that energizes trust, compassion, and common getting it. Developing weakness requires mental fortitude, self-acknowledgement, and an eagerness to share our actual selves.

Undivided attention and Compassion

Undivided attention and compassion are major practices for sustaining trust and developing profound association. Undivided attention includes really focusing, being available, and truly trying to grasp our accomplices' viewpoints and sentiments. Compassion permits us to associate with our accomplices' encounters, approving their feelings, and exhibiting understanding and backing. Undivided attention and sympathy encourage trust, advance compelling correspondence, and support a feeling of profound closeness.

Building Close to home Security

Profound wellbeing is critical for supporting trust and closeness. It includes establishing a climate where people feel open to offering their viewpoints, sentiments, and requirements unafraid of judgment or dismissal. Building close to home well being requires undivided attention, approval, and the obligation to approach each other with deference and sympathy. By encouraging profound security, we develop a climate of trust, weakness, and validness.

Recuperating Past Injuries and Changing Relationship Examples

Mending past injuries and changing relationship designs are indispensable for sustaining trust and closeness. It includes perceiving and tending to unsettled clashes, injuries, or examples of correspondence that block trust and profound association. By taking part in open discourse, looking for proficient help if necessary, and effectively dealing with self-awareness, we can mend past injuries and make better relationship elements that help trust and closeness.

Developing Appreciation and Appreciation

Developing appreciation and appreciation is a strong practice for supporting trust and extending profound association. By offering thanks for our accomplices' endeavors, characteristics, and commitments, we build up certain correspondence examples and encourage a feeling of appreciation and affirmation. Developing appreciation and appreciation improves the profound bond, reinforces trust, and cultivates a positive and strong relationship dynamic.

Respecting Limits and Assent

Regarding limits and looking for assent are fundamental for sustaining trust and making a protected and deferential relationship. Every individual has the privilege to lay out and impart their limits, and respecting them is essential. Looking for assent guarantees that activities and choices are settled on with common arrangement and regard for individual independence. Regarding limits and looking for assent exhibit trust, encourage a feeling of safety, and advance open and consensual correspondence.

Rehearsing Absolution and Empathy

Rehearsing absolution and empathy is instrumental in sustaining trust and developing profound association. Pardoning includes relinquishing hatred and feelings of resentment, permitting space for recuperating and development. Sympathy includes expanding understanding and compassion towards ourselves and our accomplices, perceiving our common humankind and questionability. By rehearsing pardoning and sympathy, we make an air of acknowledgment, understanding, and everyday encouragement.

Supporting trust and closeness is fundamental for developing solid and satisfying connections. By grasping the meaning of trust and closeness, developing weakness, rehearsing undivided attention and compassion, building profound security, recuperating past injuries, and changing relationship designs, we establish a climate that encourages profound close to home association. By developing appreciation and appreciation, regarding limits and assent, and rehearsing pardoning and empathy, we sustain trust, credibility, and shared regard. In the accompanying sections, we will dig further into explicit methods and methodologies presented by peaceful correspondence to further improve our capacity to support trust and closeness, encouraging connections that are grounded in adoration, understanding, and profound satisfaction.

CHANGING RELATIONSHIP EXAMPLES

Changing relationship designs is an essential part of quiet correspondence (PC) that permits us to make better, additional satisfying connections. In this part, we will investigate the meaning of changing relationship designs, the normal difficulties that emerge, and down to earth systems for breaking negative cycles and encouraging positive change. By understanding the elements of relationship examples and learning successful methods for change, we can develop connections that are grounded in sympathy, regard, and common development.

The Significance of Changing Relationship Examples

Changing relationship designs is fundamental for breaking patterns of contention, detachment, and disappointment. By perceiving and tending to negative examples, we can make space for better approaches for relating that cultivate figuring out, association, and cooperation. Changing relationship designs engages people to get a sense of ownership with their activities, convey all the more really, and fabricate connections

74

that are portrayed by compassion, regard, and common fulfillment.

Recognizing Negative Relationship Examples

Recognizing negative relationship designs is the most vital move toward change. These examples might appear as repeating clashes, correspondence breakdowns, or undesirable elements. By creating mindfulness and perception abilities, we can distinguish the ways of behaving, considerations, and feelings that add to pessimistic examples. Distinguishing negative examples empowers us to hinder them and set out open doors for positive change.

Getting a sense of ownership with Our Activities

Changing relationship designs requires assuming a sense of ownership with our activities and their effect on our connections. This includes recognizing the job we play in sustaining negative examples and perceiving the power we need to go with various decisions. By assuming liability, we make space for self-awareness, responsibility, and the change of our connections.

Developing Self-Sympathy and Compassion

Developing self-sympathy and compassion is fundamental during the time spent changing relationship designs. Self-empathy includes treating ourselves with graciousness and understanding, perceiving that we are untrustworthy and gaining from our missteps. Compassion permits us to comprehend and interface with the encounters and needs of others. By developing self-sympathy and sympathy, we make an establishment for empathy, understanding, and positive change in our connections.

Compelling Correspondence Strategies

Changing relationship designs requires learning and executing successful correspondence methods. These strategies incorporate undivided attention, self-assured articulation, peaceful language, and intelligent addressing. Undivided attention includes really focusing, being available, and looking to grasp the points of view and needs of others. Confident articulation permits us to plainly and consciously convey our own contemplations, sentiments, and requirements. Peaceful language includes utilizing language that advances grasping, sympathy, and joint effort. Intelligent addressing develops the discourse and welcomes self-reflection and understanding. By rehearsing these correspondence methods, we make a structure for change and positive change in our connections.

Looking for Intercession and Expert Help

Changing relationship examples might need outer help, like intervention or expert direction. Intercession can give a nonpartisan space to useful discourse and critical thinking, assisting with exploring complex relationship elements. Proficient help, for example, treatment or instructing, offers a protected and strong climate for investigating fundamental issues, acquiring bits of knowledge, and creating techniques for changing relationship designs. Looking for outer help can give important points of view, devices, and assets to work with positive change and development.

Defining Limits and Making Solid Relationship Elements

Changing relationship designs includes defining clear and sound limits. Limits characterize what is OK and what isn't seeing someone, that people's requirements and prosperity are regarded.

EXTENDING CLOSE TO HOME ASSOCIATION

Developing close to home association is a significant part of quiet correspondence (PC) that permits us to make significant and satisfying connections. In this part, we will investigate the significance of extending profound association, the hindrances that might block it, and viable techniques for developing closeness, sympathy, and close to home closeness. By grasping the elements of close to home association and applying successful procedures, we can cultivate connections that are grounded in weakness, validity, and significant association.

The Meaning of Profound Association

Profound association frames the groundwork of close and satisfying connections. It includes a profound figuring out, compassion, and reverberation with the close to home encounters of our accomplices. Profound association takes into account weakness, empathy, and the common sharing of contemplations, sentiments, and necessities. Developing close to home association enhances our connections, cultivating a feeling of having a place, understanding, and love.

Developing Presence and Care

Developing presence and care is essential for extending profound association. Presence includes being completely drawn in and mindful right now, permitting us to associate with our accomplices genuinely. Care improves our mindfulness, the capacity to appreciate people on a deeper level, and the capacity to answer as opposed to respond. By developing presence and care, we make a space for profound tuning in, sympathy, and bona fide association.

Rehearsing Empathic Tuning in

Empathic listening is a basic practice for developing profound association. It includes tuning in with an open heart and looking to grasp the feelings, necessities, and points of view of our accomplices. Empathic listening requires saving our own decisions, presumptions, and plan, and completely drenching ourselves in the experience of the other individual. By rehearsing empathic tuning in, we make a protected and strong space for profound articulation and association.

Sharing Weakness and Realness

Extending close to home association requires imparting weakness and genuineness to our accomplices. Weakness includes the eagerness to uncover our actual selves, fears, and frailties. Realness includes being veritable, legit, and straightforward in our associations. By sharing weakness and realness, we welcome our accomplices to do likewise, encouraging profound close to home association, trust, and closeness.

Building Close to home Reverberation

Building close to home reverberation includes adjusting ourselves to the profound encounters of our accomplices. It requires awareness, sympathy, and the capacity to perceive and answer inconspicuous close to home signs. Building close to home reverberation permits us to comprehend and interface with the hidden feelings of our accomplices, encouraging a profound feeling of close to home association and understanding.

Developing Ability to appreciate individuals on a profound level

Developing ability to appreciate individuals on a profound level backings the extending of close to home association. The capacity to appreciate individuals on a deeper level includes perceiving, understanding, and dealing with our own feelings and those of others. By creating the capacity to appreciate people at their core, we improve our capacity to explore profound scenes, express compassion, and impart our necessities and sentiments. Developing capacity to appreciate people on a profound level reinforces the close to home bond and cultivates profound association in connections.

Making Customs of Association

Making customs of association is a strong method for extending profound association in connections. Customs of association can be straightforward signals, exercises, or shared encounters that represent and support the close to home connection between accomplices. Models might incorporate standard date evenings, shared leisure activities, or genuine ceremonies, for example, offering thanks or participating in significant discussions. Making customs of association upgrades the feeling of closeness, euphoria, and shared significance in the relationship.

Respecting Profound Necessities

Developing profound association includes respecting the feelings of ourselves and our accomplices. This requires undivided attention, compassion, and a promise to make a protected and steady space for profound articulation. Regarding profound necessities includes approving and answering each other's feelings, giving solace and backing when required, and being mindful of the one of a kind manners by which close to home association is sustained in the relationship.

Developing Closeness Through Shared Development

Developing closeness includes embracing shared development and self-awareness inside the relationship. This might include participating in joint exercises, seeking after shared objectives, or supporting each other's singular development ventures. By effectively partaking in one another's development, we extend the profound association, encourage common help, and make a feeling of mutual perspective and satisfaction.

Extending close to home association is a groundbreaking excursion that permits us to develop connections that are wealthy in compassion, weakness, and significant association. By developing presence and care, rehearsing empathic tuning in, sharing weakness and legitimacy, and building profound reverberation, we establish a climate that encourages profound close to home association. Developing the ability to appreciate people on a deeper level, making customs of association, respecting profound requirements, and embracing shared development further upgrade the profundity of close to home association in connections. In the accompanying parts, we will dive further into explicit methods and techniques presented by quiet correspondence to further improve our capacity to develop close to home association, supporting connections that are grounded in credibility, sympathy, and love.

CHAPTER 5:

Peaceful Correspondence in Nurturing

Peaceful correspondence (PC) offers significant bits of knowledge and methods that can extraordinarily improve the nurturing experience. In this section, we will investigate the utilization of PCprinciples in nurturing, zeroing in on building sympathy with kids, settling clashes with empathy, and empowering their profound turn of events. By embracing PCin our nurturing approach, we can develop sustaining and amicable associations with our youngsters, encouraging their profound prosperity, and supporting their development.

BUILDING SYMPATHY WITH KIDS

Sympathy is a fundamental component in compelling nurturing. Building sympathy with kids includes understanding and associating with their feelings, points of view, and needs. It expects us to listen mindfully, recognize their sentiments, and approve their encounters. By rehearsing sympathy, we establish a protected and strong climate that energizes open correspondence, trust, and shared understanding.

Creating Undivided attention Abilities: Undivided attention is a central part of building sympathy with youngsters. It includes really focusing, keeping in touch, and zeroing in on grasping their contemplations and sentiments. By rehearsing undivided attention, we make space for kids to articulate their thoughts openly and feel esteemed and heard.

Approving Feelings

Approving youngsters' feelings is fundamental for building sympathy. It includes recognizing and tolerating their sentiments without judgment or analysis. Approving feelings assists kids with creating the capacity to understand people on a deeper level, mindfulness, and a feeling of profound wellbeing and acknowledgment.

Reflecting and Sympathizing

Sympathy permits us to comprehend and associate with our kids' encounters genuinely. By reflecting back their viewpoints and sentiments, we exhibit that we are sensitive to their close to home world. Identifying, imagining their perspective and envisioning how they may feel. It cultivates a profound feeling of association and empathy.

Developing Profound Mindfulness

Developing close to home mindfulness in ourselves and our youngsters is a vital part of building compassion. It includes perceiving and naming feelings, investigating their circumstances and end results, and assisting youngsters with fostering a rich close to home jargon. By advancing profound mindfulness, we enable youngsters to communicate their feelings successfully and explore them in a sound way.

Settling Clashes with Empathy

Struggle is a characteristic piece of human co-operation, including guardian kid connections. Settling clashes with sympathy permits us to address clashes such that praises everybody's necessities and fosters mutual understanding and growth. It involves shifting from a win-lose mentality to a collaborative and empathic approach.

Making a Place of refuge for Discourse

Making a safe and non-critical space for exchange is significant while settling clashes with kids. It includes carving out opportunities to examine clashes, guaranteeing that everybody feels appreciated and regarded. By making a place of refuge, we support open correspondence, sympathy, and imaginative critical thinking.

Applying Peaceful Language

Peaceful language is critical to settling clashes with sympathy. It includes utilizing language that advances grasping, regard, and association. By staying away from fault, analysis, and judgment, we make an environment that energizes cooperative critical thinking and sympathy.

Rehearsing Dynamic Critical thinking:

Dynamic critical thinking permits us to address clashes productively and cooperatively. It includes conceptualizing arrangements together, taking into account everybody's necessities, and finding mutual benefit results. By including youngsters in the critical thinking process, we show them important compromise abilities and engage them to add to positive results.

Looking for Understanding and Association

Settling clashes with sympathy requires looking for understanding and association instead of attempting to demonstrate who is correct or wrong. It includes truly paying attention to one another's viewpoints, recognizing the basic requirements and values, and settling on some shared interest. By looking for understanding and association, we develop sympathy, reinforce the parent-kid bond, and advance agreeable connections.

Empowering Profound Turn of events

Supporting youngsters' personal advancement is fundamental for their general prosperity and development. PC provides important apparatuses and techniques for sustaining the capacity to understand anyone on a profound level, self-articulation, and strength in youngsters.

Establishing a Safe Close to home Climate

Establishing a safe profound climate includes encouraging trust, acknowledgment, and open correspondence. It incorporates empowering youngsters to communicate their feelings uninhibitedly and without judgment. By making a safe close to home space, we assist kids with creating profound guideline abilities, mindfulness, and a sound connection with their feelings.

Showing Close to home Jargon

Showing youngsters an extensive profound jargon is significant for their profound turn of events. It includes presenting and naming many feelings, helping kids recognize and verbalize their sentiments. By extending their profound jargon, we engage youngsters to put themselves out there precisely, impart their requirements, and explore their feelings really.

Demonstrating sound close to home Articulation

Demonstrating solid profound articulation is a strong method for empowering youngsters' personal turn of events. It includes straightforwardly communicating our own feelings in a useful way, showing weakness, and giving a good guide to youngsters to follow. By displaying solid close to home articulation, we establish a climate that values profound validness and supports youngsters' personal development.

Empowering Self-Reflection and Sympathy

Empowering self-reflection and compassion permits kids to foster a more profound comprehension of their own feelings and the feelings of others. It includes posing intelligent inquiries, investigating the effect of their activities on others, and supporting their ability for sympathy. By encouraging self-reflection and sympathy, we advance capacity to understand people on a deeper level, empathy, and agreeable connections.

Peaceful correspondence gives a significant structure to nurturing that cultivates sympathy, compromise, and close to home improvement in youngsters. By building compassion with kids, we make major areas of strength for figuring out, association, and shared regard. Settling clashes with empathy permits us to explore clashes in a manner that advances development and reinforces the parent-kid bond. Empowering close to home advancement upholds youngsters in creating the capacity to understand people on a profound level, self-articulation, and strength. By applying PC principles in nurturing, we sustain supporting and amicable associations with our youngsters, working with their profound prosperity, and supporting their development. In the accompanying sections, we will dive further into explicit procedures and methodologies presented by peaceful correspondence for successful nurturing, engaging us to establish a sustaining and strong climate for our kids' turn of events.

BUILDING COMPASSION WITH KIDS

Building compassion with kids is a central part of peaceful correspondence (PC) that encourages figuring out, association, and profound prosperity. In this section, we will investigate the significance of compassion in nurturing, the advantages it brings to youngsters' turn of events, and useful systems for developing sympathy. By embracing compassion, we can establish a sustaining and steady climate that permits youngsters to flourish genuinely and socially.

The Meaning of Compassion in Nurturing

Sympathy is the capacity to comprehend and discuss the thoughts of someone else. In nurturing, compassion assumes a critical part in major areas of strength for building with kids and advancing their profound turn of events. It permits guardians to interface with their youngsters on a more profound level, approve their feelings, and answer their requirements with sympathy and understanding. By rehearsing sympathy, guardians make a place of refuge for youngsters to communicate their thoughts, cultivating trust, confidence, and solid close to home guidelines.

Creating Profound Mindfulness

Creating close to home mindfulness is a key stage in building sympathy with kids. It includes perceiving and grasping our own feelings as well as those of our kids. By developing close to home mindfulness, guardians can adjust themselves to their youngsters' personal states, actually approving and answering their sentiments. Profound mindfulness permits guardians to interface with their kids' encounters and offer help in a delicate and sympathetic way.

Undivided attention and Intelligent Correspondence

Undivided attention and intelligent correspondence are fundamental apparatuses for building compassion with kids. Undivided attention includes concentrating on our kids, both verbally and non-verbally. It requires being available, keeping in touch, and really looking to grasp their viewpoints and feelings. Intelligent correspondence includes rewording and summing up what kids express, mirroring their considerations and sentiments back to them. By rehearsing undivided attention and intelligent correspondence, guardians show their readiness to comprehend and approve their kids' encounters, encouraging a profound feeling of compassion and association.

Approving Feelings

Approving feelings is a strong method for building compassion with youngsters. It includes recognizing and tolerating their feelings without judgment or analysis. By approving youngsters' feelings, guardians impart that their sentiments are perceived and acknowledged, advancing a feeling of close to home security and trust. Approving feelings additionally assists kids with creating the capacity to understand anyone on a profound level, mindfulness, and the capacity to really control their feelings.

Developing Empathic Language

Developing empathic language is instrumental in building compassion with kids. Empathic language includes utilizing words and expressions that convey figuring out, sympathy, and association. It incorporates expressions, for example, "I can see that you're not kidding.." "It seems as though you're profoundly vexed about...". By utilizing empathic language, guardians exhibit their empathic comprehension and make a scaffold of association with their kids, empowering them to communicate their feelings all the more unreservedly and straightforwardly.

Displaying Sympathy

Displaying sympathy is a strong method for showing kids compassion and cultivating its turn of events. Guardians can display sympathy by exhibiting figuring out, empathy, and regard in their connections with their kids and others. By demonstrating sympathy, guardians give a substantial illustration of empathic way of behaving, permitting youngsters to notice and assimilate empathic reactions in their own collaborations.

Empowering Viewpoint Taking

Empowering viewpoint taking assists kids with creating compassion by permitting them to see circumstances from various perspectives. Guardians can energize point of view taking by posing inquiries that welcome kids to consider how others may be feeling or thinking. By drawing in youngsters in context taking activities, guardians develop their capacity to comprehend and feel for the encounters of others.

Showing Caring Critical thinking

Showing merciful critical thinking includes directing youngsters in tracking down arrangements that address everybody's issues and advance shared understanding. It urges kids to consider the sentiments and necessities of others while communicating their own. By including youngsters in cooperative critical thinking, guardians support their empathic abilities and engage them to take part in valuable and merciful collaborations.

Developing Empathy Through Shared Encounters

Developing compassion through shared encounters gives potential open doors to kids to foster sympathy by interfacing with others and figuring out their encounters. Guardians can take part in exercises that advance sympathy, for example, chipping in together or taking part in agreeable games and ventures. By partaking in shared encounters, kids figure out how to understand others, appreciate alternate points of view, and foster a feeling of social obligation.

Building sympathy with youngsters is an extraordinary part of nurturing that sustains their close to home prosperity, encourages association, and advances solid social turn of events. By creating close to home mindfulness, rehearsing undivided attention and intelligent correspondence, approving feelings, developing empathic language, and displaying sympathy, guardians establish an empathic climate that upholds youngsters' personal development. Empowering viewpoint taking, showing empathetic critical thinking, and developing empathy through

SETTLING CLASHES WITH EMPATHY

Struggle is a characteristic piece of human corporations, and it is the same in the parent-kid relationship. Settling clashes with empathy is a crucial part of quiet correspondence (PC) that permits guardians to address clashes such that sustains figuring out, regard, and association. In this part, we will investigate the significance of settling clashes with sympathy, the difficulties that might emerge, and down to earth methodologies for exploring clashes in a peaceful and helpful way.

Understanding Clash in Nurturing

Struggle in nurturing emerges from contrasts in requirements, assumptions, and viewpoints among guardians and youngsters. It can happen in different regions, like everyday schedules, discipline, or navigation. Understanding clash as a chance for development and learning permits guardians to move toward clashes with an empathetic mentality, looking for a goal as opposed to trying to win or rule.

Establishing a Protected and Conscious Climate

Establishing a protected and deferential climate is critical while settling clashes with sympathy. It includes laying out clear limits for deferential correspondence, for example, abstaining from shouting, ridiculing, or actual hostility. By making a place of refuge, guardians give an establishment to transparent exchange, cultivating understanding and trust.

Rehearsing Undivided attention

Undivided attention is a crucial practice in settling clashes with sympathy. It includes concentrating completely on the speaker, suspending judgment, and looking to grasp their point of view and hidden needs. By rehearsing undivided attention, guardians exhibit their obligation to figure out their youngsters' perspectives, encouraging compassion and association.

Communicating Requirements and Sentiments

Communicating requirements and sentiments in a helpful and peaceful way is fundamental in settling clashes. It includes utilizing "I" proclamations to communicate feelings and requirements, for example, "I feel..." and "I need...". By communicating needs and sentiments, guardians make an environment of open correspondence, permitting kids to share their own points of view and needs.

Looking for Shared benefit Arrangements

Settling clashes with empathy requires looking for mutual benefit arrangements that address the issues of all gatherings included. It includes conceptualizing and investigating inventive choices that honor everybody's requirements. By focusing on joint effort and participation over battles for control, guardians cultivate a feeling of reasonableness and common regard in compromise.

Applying Peaceful Language

Peaceful language is instrumental in settling clashes with empathy. It includes utilizing language that advances figuring out, compassion, and association. By abstaining from accusing, censuring, or disgracing language, guardians establish a climate that empowers helpful discourse and critical thinking.

Settling on some shared interest

Figuring out something worth agreeing on is a fundamental part of settling clashes with sympathy. It includes recognizing shared interests or objectives that can act as a reason for tracking down commonly fulfilling arrangements. By zeroing in on areas of arrangement, guardians can connect contrasts and work cooperatively towards a goal.

Showing Compromise Abilities

Showing compromise abilities to youngsters enables them to explore clashes in an empathetic and peaceful way. It includes furnishing them with instruments and procedures for communicating their necessities, effectively tuning in, and looking for shared benefit arrangements. By showing compromise abilities, guardians furnish their youngsters with fundamental abilities that advance sound connections and compelling correspondence.

Rehearsing Absolution and Fix

Rehearsing absolution and fix is pivotal in settling clashes with empathy. It includes recognizing botches, assuming liability, and offering veritable statements of regret. By rehearsing pardoning and fixing, guardians make a culture of responsibility, sympathy, and recuperating inside the parent-kid relationship.

Settling clashes with empathy is a basic piece of nurturing that supports figuring out, regard, and association. By establishing a protected and deferential climate, rehearsing undivided attention, communicating necessities and sentiments, looking for mutual benefit arrangements, and applying peaceful language, guardians encourage a productive way to deal with compromise. Figuring out something worth agreeing on, showing compromise abilities, and rehearsing, pardoning and fixing further improve the goal interaction. By embracing struggle as a chance for development and learning, guardians establish a climate where clashes can be tended to with sympathy, understanding, and empathy. In the accompanying parts, we will dig further into explicit methods and systems presented by peaceful correspondence to further upgrade our capacity to determine clashes with empathy, advancing amicable and sustaining associations with our youngsters.

Empowering Close to Home Turn of Events

Profound improvement is a basic part of kids' general prosperity and outcome throughout everyday life. tranquil correspondence (PC) gives important apparatuses and approaches that can uphold guardians in cultivating their youngsters' personal turn of events. In this part, we will investigate the significance of close to home turn of events, the difficulties that might emerge, and commonsense systems for empowering profound development in kids. By embracing PCprinciples, guardians can establish a sustaining climate that advances the capacity to understand people at their core, self-articulation, and flexibility.

Figuring out Close to home Turn of events

Close to home advancement alludes to the development and development of youngsters' personal limits, including their capacity to perceive, comprehend, and deal with their own feelings and understand others. It includes creating close to home mindfulness, guideline abilities, and a sound connection with feelings. Understanding the phases of close to home improvement permits guardians to offer proper help and direction to their kids.

Empowering Self-Reflection and Compassion

Empowering self-reflection and compassion permits kids to foster a more profound comprehension of their own feelings and the feelings of others. It includes posing intelligent inquiries, investigating the effect of their activities on others, and sustaining their ability for sympathy. By cultivating self-reflection and sympathy, guardians advance capacity to understand people on a profound level, empathy, and agreeable connections.

Offering Close to home Help

Offering close to home help is fundamental in empowering youngsters' personal turn of events. It includes being receptive to their feelings, offering solace, and giving a listening ear. By being available and receptive to their profound encounters, guardians make a feeling of safety, trust, and close to home prosperity in their youngsters.

Showing Profound Guideline Abilities

Showing youngsters close to home guideline abilities is urgent for their profound turn of events. It includes giving them systems for overseeing and communicating their feelings in solid ways. By showing methods like profound breathing, positive self-talk, and care, guardians enable youngsters to explore testing feelings and foster strength.

Developing Capacity to understand people at their core

Developing the capacity to understand people on a profound level is a deep rooted excursion, and guardians assume a huge part in this cycle. The ability to appreciate people on a deeper level includes perceiving, understanding, and dealing with feelings successfully, as well as relating to the feelings of others. By supporting the capacity to understand people at their core, guardians furnish youngsters with fundamental abilities for building solid connections, settling on informed choices, and overseeing pressure.

Commending and Approving Feelings

Commending and approving kids' feelings is fundamental in empowering their close to home turn of events. It includes recognizing and valuing the full scope of feelings kids insight, including both good and gloomy feelings. By commending and approving their feelings, guardians make a culture of profound acknowledgment and backing, cultivating confidence and close to home prosperity.

Empowering profound improvement is a groundbreaking part of nurturing that supports kids' personal prosperity, self-articulation, and flexibility. By establishing a sincerely steady climate, showing close to home jargon, demonstrating solid profound articulation, and empowering self-reflection and sympathy, guardians establish the groundwork for profound development. Offering close to home help, showing profound guideline abilities, and developing capacity to appreciate people at their core further upgrade youngsters' personal turn of events.

CHAPTER 6:

Peaceful Correspondence in the Working Environment

The working environment is a unique climate where successful correspondence is fundamental for efficiency, joint effort, and a positive hierarchical culture. In this section, we will investigate the use of quiet correspondence (PC) standards in the working environment setting. By integrating PC techniques, people can improve their relational abilities, resolve clashes helpfully, and create a culture of sympathy and trust. This part plans to give reasonable systems and experiences to using PCto further develop working environment cooperations and cultivate an agreeable workplace.

The Significance of peaceful correspondence in the Working environment

peaceful correspondence offers a strong structure for tending to working environment challenges and advancing solid connections among partners. It underscores empathic grasping, non-critical correspondence, and the capacity to communicate needs and concerns really. By rehearsing PC, people can cultivate a deferential and comprehensive working environment culture that values open correspondence, joint effort, and self-improvement.

Improving Relational abilities in the Working environment

Viable correspondence is the foundation of fruitful work connections and collaboration. PC provides significant apparatuses for upgrading relational abilities in the work environment.

Undivided attention

Undivided attention is a basic part of viable correspondence. It includes concentrating completely on the speaker, suspending judgment, and trying to grasp their viewpoint. By effectively tuning in, people can cultivate compassion, fabricate trust, and advance a culture of open correspondence.

Clear and Aware Articulation

Clear and deferential articulation includes utilizing peaceful language, offering viewpoints and needs emphatically, and giving useful criticism. By imparting plainly and consciously, people can keep away from errors, advance comprehension, and assemble more grounded associations with partners.

Nonverbal Correspondence

Nonverbal signals, like non-verbal communication and looks, assume a critical part in working environment correspondence. PC emphasizes the significance of monitoring and answering nonverbal prompts, as they can convey feelings and aims. By focusing on nonverbal correspondence, people can improve understanding and advance powerful correspondence.

Settling Clashes and Cooperation in the Working environment

Clashes are unavoidable in the working environment, yet they can potentially open doors for development and cooperation when drawn closer with tranquil correspondence standards.

Cooperative Critical thinking

PC promotes cooperative critical thinking for settling clashes. By empowering open discourse, effectively paying attention to all gatherings included, and looking for shared benefit arrangements, people can encourage a culture of joint effort and cooperation. Cooperative critical thinking considers the investigation of effective fixes that address the basic requirements and worries, everything being equal.

Intercession and Facilitation

In more perplexing or raised clashes, the contribution of an unbiased outsider prepared in PC can be valuable. Intervention or help gives an organized interaction to settling clashes, guaranteeing that every one of gatherings' voices are heard, and directing the correspondence towards a commonly palatable goal.

Making Sympathy and Confidence in the Work environment

Sympathy and trust are critical for laying out a positive workplace and building solid connections among partners.

Developing Empathy

PC emphasizes the development of sympathy as an essential component of viable correspondence. By effectively looking to grasp the feelings, requirements, and points of view of others, people can cultivate compassion and make a strong working environment culture. Sympathy empowers people to interface on a more profound level, form trust, and reinforce connections.

Building Trust

Trust is worked through predictable and straightforward correspondence, dependability, and common regard. PCencourages people to rehearse uprightness, validity, and undivided attention to lay out trust in the work environment. By regarding responsibilities, being responsible for activities, and approaching associates with deference, people can cultivate trust and establish a climate where transparent correspondence can flourish.

Empowering a Culture of Sympathy and Trust

Making a culture of compassion and trust requires progressing exertion and responsibility from all individuals from the association. PC principles can direct people in advancing compassion and trust by empowering open correspondence, regarding assorted points of view, and esteeming the commitments of each colleague. By encouraging a culture of sympathy and trust, associations can establish a climate that supports cooperation, development, and representative prosperity.

quiet correspondence offers important experiences and strategies for improving relational abilities, settling clashes, and making compassion and confidence in the working environment. By integrating PC principles into work environment connections, people can encourage aware and helpful correspondence, resolve clashes cooperatively, and fabricate solid connections in view of sympathy and trust. The use of PCs in the working environment advances a positive hierarchical culture, upgrades cooperation, and adds to individual and hierarchical achievement. In the accompanying parts, we will dig further into explicit uses of PCin the working environment, tending to subjects like authority, group elements, and authoritative change.

Upgrading Relational abilities

Powerful correspondence is the underpinning of effective connections, both individual and expert. In the working, serious areas of strength for environment abilities are pivotal for building compatibility, encouraging joint effort, and accomplishing authoritative objectives. peaceful correspondence (PC) offers down to earth apparatuses and procedures that can improve relational abilities and advance positive and helpful corporations. In this part, we will investigate different parts of correspondence and how PC principles can be applied to improve relational abilities in the work environment.

Undivided attention

Undivided attention is a fundamental part of viable correspondence. It includes completely captivating with the speaker, figuring out their message, and answering in a way that exhibits sympathy and understanding. Undivided attention requires really focusing on the speaker. This implies limiting interruptions, for example, switching off electronic gadgets and keeping in touch. By showing certified interest and mindfulness, you establish a climate that energizes transparent correspondence.

Verbal and Nonverbal Cues

Active listening includes utilizing verbal and nonverbal prompts to show that you are effectively participating in the discussion. Gesturing, keeping an open body stance, and utilizing fitting looks are nonverbal signs that demonstrate mindfulness and understanding. Verbal signs, for example, rewording or summing up the speaker's message, help to explain understanding and exhibit that you are effectively tuning in.

Empathic Comprehension

Empathic comprehension is a vital part of undivided attention. It includes imagining the speaker's perspective, attempting to grasp their point of view, and approving their sentiments and encounters. By exhibiting sympathy, you make a place of refuge for transparent correspondence, encouraging trust and more profound associations with partners.

Peaceful Language

The utilization of peaceful language is significant for successful correspondence and keeping up with positive connections in the work environment. PCemphasizes the significance of picking words and articulations that are aware, non-accusing, and non-critical.

Use "I" Proclamations: "I" explanations are an incredible asset for offering viewpoints, sentiments, and requirements without accusing or denouncing others. By utilizing "I" explanations, you get a sense of ownership with your feelings and abstain from finding fault with others, cultivating a non-fierce climate.

Stay away from Analysis and Judgment

PC encourages people to stay away from analysis, judgment, and pessimistic language in their correspondence. Rather than zeroing in on flaws or deficiencies, center around unambiguous ways of behaving or circumstances. By abstaining from judgment, you make an environment that advances understanding and coordinated effort.

Look for Lucidity and Understanding

Successful correspondence requires clearness. On the off chance that something is muddled or questionable, looking for clarification is fundamental. Pose unassuming inquiries and effectively pay attention to guarantee a common perspective. By looking for clearness, you can forestall misconceptions and advance powerful correspondence.

Careful and Insightful Correspondence

Careful correspondence includes monitoring your words and their effect on others. It requires insightful thought of how your message might be gotten. By rehearsing careful correspondence, you can proceed with caution, keep away from hasty or pernicious comments, and advance a positive and conscious climate.

Decisiveness and Communicating Needs

Decisiveness is a significant part of powerful correspondence. It includes offering your viewpoints, necessities, and limits in an unmistakable and certain way while regarding the freedoms and points of view of others.

Offering Viewpoints and Thoughts

Compelling correspondence expects people to offer their viewpoints and thoughts plainly and certainly. By articulating your perspectives, you add to open conversations and advance different viewpoints in the work environment. Make sure to listen effectively and be available to others' thoughts too.

Defining Limits

Limits are fundamental for keeping up with sound work connections. Conveying your limits self-assuredly lays out assumptions and guarantees that your necessities are met. By defining limits, you establish a workplace that regards individual cutoff points and advances generally speaking prosperity.

Giving Productive Input

Useful criticism is a significant device for development and improvement. While giving input, center around unambiguous ways of behaving, be elucidating as opposed to critical, and give ideas for development. By giving helpful criticism, you make a strong and development situated work culture.

Dynamic Critical thinking

Viable correspondence includes dynamic critical thinking. Team up with partners to track down arrangements, conceptualize thoughts, and look for mutual benefit results. By taking part in dynamic critical thinking, you advance cooperation, assemble more grounded connections, and accomplish improved results.

Upgrading relational abilities is significant for viable and amicable work environment collaborations. By integrating PC principles, like undivided attention, utilizing peaceful language, and communicating needs self-assuredly, people can further develop their relational abilities and establish a positive workplace. Viable correspondence works with understanding, forms trust, and cultivates joint effort among associates. By putting time and exertion into improving relational abilities, people can add to their self-improvement, proficient turn of events, and the general progress of the association. In the accompanying parts, we will investigate extra parts of tranquil correspondence in the working environment, like compromise, compassion, and trust-working, to additional upgrade correspondence and connections inside the workplace.

SETTLING STRUGGLE AND COORDINATED EFFORT

Struggle is a characteristic piece of human connection, and it can emerge in any working environment setting. Be that as it may, what clashes are taken care of and settled can essentially mean for the workplace and efficiency. Peaceful correspondence (PC) gives a structure to settling clashes in a useful and humane way, advancing joint effort and keeping up with positive connections. In this part, we will investigate the use of PC principles in settling clashes and cultivating joint effort in the work environment.

Grasping Clash

Struggle can emerge according to contrasting points of view, requirements, or objectives among people or groups in the work environment. It is fundamental to perceive that contention isn't intrinsically negative yet a chance for development and improvement. Understanding the underlying drivers and elements of contention is the most important move toward settling it successfully.

Distinguishing Hidden Needs

Struggle frequently arises when people's necessities are not being met. PC emphasizes the significance of recognizing and recognizing these fundamental requirements. By understanding the requirements of all gatherings included, people can pursue tracking down commonly palatable arrangements.

Perceiving Damaging Examples

Struggle can become disastrous in the event that it is drawn closer with hostility, fault, or a success lose mindset. PC encourages people to perceive and break these damaging examples by taking on a peaceful and cooperative way to deal with compromise.

Seeing Clash as an Open door

PC reframes struggle as a chance for development, learning, and reinforcing connections. By embracing struggle as an opportunity to comprehend others better, investigate clever fixes, and encourage coordinated effort, people can change clashes into impetuous for positive change.

Peaceful Compromise

Peaceful compromise includes applying PC principles and strategies to address clashes in a humane and productive way. It centers around finding mutual benefit arrangements that address the issues of all gatherings included.

Making a Place of refuge for Discourse

A protected and steady climate is fundamental for compelling compromise. PCencourages people to make such a space by guaranteeing that all gatherings feel appreciated, regarded, and liberated from judgment. This place of refuge takes into account transparent exchange, encouraging comprehension and sympathy.

Undivided attention and Sympathy

Undivided attention and compassion are key parts of peaceful compromise. By listening mindfully and looking to figure out the points of view, necessities, and feelings of others, people can show sympathy and encourage a more profound association. This assists with building trust and makes an establishment for successful compromise.

Communicating Sentiments and Requirements

PC encourages people to communicate their sentiments and necessities in a reasonable and non-accusing way during compromise. By utilizing "I" proclamations and zeroing in on private encounters, people can convey their feelings and needs actually, advancing comprehension and sympathy.

Cooperative Critical thinking

Peaceful compromise includes cooperative critical thinking. By connecting all gatherings simultaneously and looking for savvy fixes, people can find mutual benefit results that address the fundamental requirements and worries of all interested parties. Cooperative critical thinking encourages collaboration, reinforces connections, and advances a positive work culture.

Intercession and Help

At times, clashes might require the intercession of a nonpartisan outsider to work with a goal. Intercession and help, in light of PC principles, give an organized and steady climate for settling clashes.

Intercession

Intervention includes the contribution of an impartial go between who directs the compromise cycle. The middle person works with correspondence, guarantees that all gatherings are heard, and assists people with investigating commonly pleasant arrangements.

Intervention advances grasping, compassion, and coordinated effort, prompting economical goals.

Help

Assistance alludes to the method involved with directing cooperative conversations to determine clashes. A gifted facilitator prepared in PC principles can make a place of refuge for open exchange, support undivided attention, and cultivate useful correspondence. Assistance assists people with figuring out something worth agreeing on and making progress toward commonly useful goals.

Cultivating Coordinated effort

Joint effort is fundamental for a fruitful and useful work environment. PC principles can assist with encouraging a cooperative workplace by advancing viable correspondence, common regard, and shared liability.

Open Correspondence and Straightforwardness

Cooperation flourishes in a climate of open correspondence and straightforwardness. PC encourages people to share data, thoughts, and concerns transparently. By advancing a culture of straightforwardness, people can cooperate all the more really and settle on informed choices.

Esteeming Assorted Viewpoints

Joint effort benefits from the consideration of different viewpoints and thoughts. PC emphasizes the significance of esteeming and regarding the commitments of all colleagues, no matter what their experiences or positions. By embracing variety and establishing a comprehensive workplace, people can use various perspectives and improve joint effort.

Laying out Shared objectives

Joint effort is fortified when all gatherings are making progress toward a shared objective. PC encourages people to distinguish and express shared objectives and targets. By adjusting endeavors, people can cooperate all the more actually, pooling their abilities and assets to accomplish normal results.

Advancing Collaboration and Participation

PC principles advance collaboration and collaboration by encouraging a feeling of shared liability and common help. By empowering people to team up, share information, and assist each other, a culture of collaboration with canning be developed. This adds to a good workplace where partners feel upheld and esteemed.

Settling clashes and encouraging cooperation are essential for keeping a positive and useful workplace. By applying PC principles, people can move toward clashes with compassion, look for mutual benefit arrangements, and assemble solid connections in light of trust and understanding. Peaceful compromise empowers open and valuable discourse, prompting further developed correspondence, collaboration, and generally speaking authoritative achievement. Encouraging joint effort through viable correspondence, esteeming different viewpoints, and advancing cooperation establishes a workplace where people can flourish and add to shared objectives. By integrating PC principles into compromise and cooperation endeavors, people can change clashes into open doors for development, advancement, and more grounded connections. In the accompanying parts, we will investigate extra parts of quiet correspondence in the working environment, including sympathy building and trust-working, to additional help compromise and cooperation.

MAKING COMPASSION AND TRUST

Compassion and trust are fundamental components of significant and satisfying connections, both by and by and expertly. In the work environment, developing compassion and trust is pivotal for establishing a positive workplace, cultivating coordinated effort, and upgrading in general efficiency. peaceful correspondence (PC) gives significant experiences and practices that can assist people foster sympathy and construct entrust in their cooperations with partners. In this section, we will investigate the ideas of compassion and trust, their importance in the work environment, and how PC principles can be applied to develop and sustain these fundamental parts of viable correspondence.

Grasping Sympathy

Compassion is the capacity to comprehend and discuss the thoughts, viewpoints, and encounters of others. It includes imagining another person's perspective and seeing the world according to their perspective. In the work environment, compassion assumes an imperative part in building compatibility, encouraging comprehension, and advancing agreeable connections.

Undivided attention and Presence: Undivided attention is a vital part of sympathy. By really focusing, being completely present, and genuinely standing by listening to other people, you show that their contemplations and sentiments matter. This approves their encounters and encourages a more profound feeling of association.

Point of view Taking

Viewpoint taking is the act of envisioning oneself in someone else's circumstance. By taking into account their contemplations, feelings, and inspirations, people can acquire bits of knowledge into their point of view and foster a more noteworthy comprehension of their encounters. Viewpoint advances sympathy by perceiving the exceptional difficulties and conditions looked by others.

Non-Critical Demeanor

Compassion requires suspending judgment and taking on a non-critical disposition. By ceasing from assessing or censuring others, people make a place of refuge for transparent correspondence. This permits associates to share their contemplations, sentiments, and worries unafraid of judgment or revenge.

Approval and Affirmation

Sympathy includes approving and recognizing the sentiments and encounters of others. By communicating understanding and sympathy, people exhibit that they value and regard the feelings and points of view of their partners. Approval cultivates trust and establishes a steady workplace.

Building Trust

Trust is the underpinning of fruitful connections and is crucial in the working environment for cooperation, viable collaboration, and open correspondence. Building trust requires consistency, honesty, and a guarantee to straightforwardness and regard.

Dependability and Consistency

Trust is based on the groundwork of unwavering quality and consistency. People who reliably satisfy their responsibilities, comply with time constraints, and keep their word are seen as dependable. By showing dependability, people impart trust in their associates and assemble trust.

Straightforwardness and Open Correspondence

Trust flourishes in a climate of straightforwardness and open correspondence. PC encourages people to share data, offer viewpoints and concerns sincerely, and participate in productive exchange. Straightforward correspondence encourages trust by guaranteeing that everybody approaches significant data and advances a feeling of decency and incorporation.

Regarding Limits and Classification

Trust is firmly connected to regarding limits and keeping up with secrecy. Regarding the protection and secrecy of partners fabricates trust and lays out a protected climate where people feel open to sharing their considerations, concerns, and thoughts. By regarding limits, people exhibit regard and make a climate of trust.

Reliable Criticism and Backing

Giving steady input and backing is fundamental for building trust. By offering valuable criticism, perceiving accomplishments, and giving direction and help when required, people show their interest in the development and improvement of their partners. Steady input and backing foster trust and establish a climate that advances learning and cooperation.

APPLYING PC FOR DEVELOPING SYMPATHY AND TRUST

PC gives significant standards and practices to developing compassion and confidence in the working environment. By coordinating PC into everyday associations, people can establish a climate that advances grasping, compassion, and trust.

Peaceful Language

Peaceful language is a center part of PC and adds to the development of sympathy and trust. By utilizing non-accusing and non-critical language, people make a place of refuge for open correspondence. Peaceful language urges partners to communicate their thoughts sincerely and advances a culture of understanding and regard.

Undivided attention and Intelligent Reactions

Undivided attention, joined with intelligent reactions, extends compassion and trust. By effectively standing by listening to other people, people can show their advantage and obligation to grasping their partners' points of view. Intelligent reactions, for example, rewording or summing up, show that people have perceived and recognized the speaker's message, encouraging trust and reinforcing associations.

Compromise with Empathy

Struggle is unavoidable in the work environment, however settling clashes with sympathy is vital to keeping up with trust and encouraging positive connections. PC provides systems for tending to clashes in a peaceful and helpful way. By moving toward clashes with compassion, effectively paying attention to all gatherings included, and looking for mutual benefit arrangements, people can determine clashes while keeping up with trust and safeguarding connections.

Sympathy Building Activities

PC offers compassion building practices that can be drilled in the working environment. These activities incorporate point of view taking, pretending, and gathering conversations zeroed in on figuring out the encounters and feelings of associates. By taking part in compassion building works out, people foster a more profound comprehension of each other and fortify their capacity to identify associates.

Sympathy and trust are significant resources in the working environment, adding to the formation of a positive workplace, encouraging cooperation, and improving generally speaking efficiency. By coordinating PC standards into everyday collaborations, people can develop sympathy, construct trust, and make significant associations with partners. Undivided attention, point of view taking, peaceful language, and compromise with sympathy are key practices in cultivating compassion and trust. The improvement of these abilities requires predictable exertion and a promise to establish a climate where compassion and trust can flourish. By focusing on compassion and trust, associations can cultivate a culture of open correspondence, coordinated effort, and shared help, bringing about expanded work fulfillment, further developed cooperation, and improved general achievement. In the accompanying parts, we will investigate extra parts of quiet correspondence in the working environment, including administration and hierarchical culture, to further help the development of compassion and trust.

PART III
APPLYING PEACEFUL CORRESPONDENCE IN DAILY LIFE

CHAPTER 7:
Developing
SELF-Sympathy

Self-empathy is a strong practice that permits people to foster generosity, understanding, and acknowledgment towards themselves. With regards to peaceful correspondence (PC), self-sympathy is fundamental for encouraging self-awareness, keeping up with profound prosperity, and further developing correspondence with others. In this part, we will investigate the idea of self-sympathy and its importance with regards to PC. We will dig into useful procedures and strategies that can assist people develop self-empathy and foster a better relationship with themselves.

Figuring out Self-Sympathy

Self-sympathy includes treating oneself with graciousness, care, and understanding, particularly during testing or troublesome minutes. It is tied in with recognizing one's own humankind, embracing flaws, and offering oneself the very sympathy and backing that one would reach out to other people. With regards to PC, self-sympathy is a major part of carrying on with a peaceful and empathic life.

Self-Acknowledgment and Non-Judgment

Self-sympathy starts with self-acknowledgement. It includes relinquishing self-judgment, self-analysis, and the requirement for flawlessness. PC teaches people to develop self-acknowledgement by perceiving that all people have needs, commit errors, and experience difficulties. By rethinking self-judgment into self-acknowledgment, people can cultivate a merciful outlook towards themselves.

Graciousness and Understanding

Self-empathy involves treating oneself with consideration and figuring out, even in troublesome conditions. It includes offering oneself the very backing and care that one would reach out to a dear companion or cherished one. PC encourages people to foster a sustaining and steady relationship with themselves, which incorporates answering their own necessities with sympathy and understanding.

Care and Mindfulness:

Self-empathy is personally associated with care and mindfulness. By developing a present-second mindfulness and noticing one's considerations, feelings, and actual sensations without judgment, people can foster a more noteworthy comprehension of their own encounters. Care empowers people to answer their own requirements and difficulties with sympathy and taking care of oneself.

The Job of Self-Sympathy in PC

Self-sympathy is profoundly interwoven with the standards and practices of PC. It is the establishment whereupon peaceful correspondence with others is assembled. Without self-sympathy, people might battle to broaden compassion, understanding, and acknowledgment to other people.

Profound Guideline and Sympathy

Self-empathy upholds close to home guidelines and compassion. By recognizing and approving one's own feelings, people can develop a more profound comprehension of their own requirements and encounters. This mindfulness then empowers people to relate to other people, perceiving and approving their feelings and necessities in a caring way.

Peaceful Language and Internal Discourse

Self-sympathy impacts the internal exchange and self-talk that people participate in. PC principles guide people to utilize peaceful language and caring self-talk while tending to their own necessities, difficulties, and self-saw inadequacies. By rehearsing peaceful self-talk, people cultivate self-acknowledgement, graciousness, and consolation.

Flexibility and Development Outlook

Self-sympathy adds to strength and a development mentality. By moving toward difficulties with self-sympathy, people can see mishaps as any open doors for learning and development instead of individual disappointments. PC encourages people to embrace mix-ups and difficulties as a component of the educational experience and to answer with self-sympathy and a development situated mentality.

Methodologies for Developing Self-Sympathy

Developing self-empathy is a continuous practice that requires goal, tolerance, and self-reflection. PC offers a few procedures and methods that people can utilize to develop self-sympathy in their lives.

Careful Self-Sympathy Contemplation

Careful self-empathy reflection includes saving devoted time for self-reflection and self-empathy rehearses. This can remember centering for the breath, offering kind and strong words to oneself, or envisioning a sympathetic presence. Normal reflection assists people with fostering a propensity for self-sympathy and expands their ability to answer with thoughtfulness and understanding.

Taking care of oneself and Self-Supporting

Participating in taking care of oneself exercises is a fundamental part of self-sympathy. PC encourages people to focus on self-sustaining rehearsals that line up with their requirements and values. This can incorporate taking part in exercises that give pleasure, unwinding, and restoration, like investing energy in nature, rehearsing leisure activities, or looking for social help.

Self-Reflection and Journaling

Self-reflection and journaling give valuable open doors to people to investigate their considerations, feelings, and encounters in a non-critical and empathetic manner. PC encourages people to take part in self-reflection rehearsals, like writing in an appreciation diary or considering snapshots of self-empathy over the course of the day. This self-reflection encourages mindfulness and develops the act of self-sympathy.

Looking for Help

Looking for help from confided in companions, guides, or specialists can be instrumental in developing self-empathy. PC emphasizes the significance of association and cooperation, and looking for help from others lines up with these standards. Participating in open and empathic discussions with strong people can give approval, point of view, and consolation in the excursion of self-sympathy.

Developing self-empathy is a groundbreaking practice that empowers people to foster a kinder and really tolerating relationship with themselves. With regards to PC, self-empathy is a principal part of carrying on with a peaceful and empathic life. By embracing self-acknowledgement, offering oneself consideration and understanding, and participating in taking care of oneself practices, people can cultivate a humane outlook and stretch out compassion and understanding to other people. Developing self-empathy requires steady exertion, self-reflection, and a guarantee to self-awareness. By coordinating self-empathy into day to day existence, people can upgrade their profound prosperity, work on their correspondence with others, and add to a positive and sustaining workplace. In the accompanying parts, we will investigate extra parts of Peaceful Correspondence, including authority, cooperation, and compromise, to further help self-awareness and empathic associations in the working environment.

CHANGING SELF-ANALYSIS

Self-analysis is a typical and frequently profoundly imbued propensity that can obstruct self-improvement, self-acknowledgement, and by and large prosperity. With regards to peaceful correspondence (PC), changing self-analysis includes developing self-sympathy, embracing compassion, and moving towards an outlook of development and self-acknowledgement. In this section, we will investigate the idea of self-analysis, its effect on people's lives, and viable procedures for changing self-analysis into self-empathy utilizing PC principles.

Grasping Self-Analysis

Self-analysis is the propensity to pass judgment, condemn, and upbraid oneself for saw weaknesses, missteps, or disappointments. It frequently comes from incorporated cultural assumptions, examination with others, or a longing for flawlessness. While it could be driven by the goal to improve, self-analysis will in general be cruel, useless, and impeding one's prosperity.

Distinguishing proof and Mindfulness

The most important phase in changing self-analysis is to recognize and become mindful of self-decisive contemplations and examples. PC encourages people to notice their internal discourse, perceive self-judgment, and carry empathetic attention to these contemplations.

Perceiving the Effect

Self-analysis influences confidence, certainty, and close to home prosperity. It can make a pattern of pessimism, prompting pressure, tension, and even misery. Understanding the effect of self-analysis is vital in developing the inspiration to change it into a more sympathetic and development situated mentality.

Testing Unreasonable Principles:

Self-analysis frequently emerges from ridiculous norms and assumptions. PC encourages people to challenge these norms and embrace a more practical and humane perspective on themselves. It includes perceiving and esteeming one's assets, celebrating progress, and recognizing that errors and defects are a characteristic piece of the human experience.

Developing Self-Empathy

Changing self-analysis includes developing self-empathy, which is the act of treating oneself with generosity, understanding, and acknowledgment. PC offers significant systems and strategies to cultivate self-sympathy and shift towards a more empathetic and development situated outlook.

Rehearsing Self-Acknowledgment

Self-acknowledgement is a central part of self-empathy. PC encourages people to recognize and acknowledge themselves, including their assets, shortcomings, and flaws. By rehearsing self-acknowledgement, people can relinquish the requirement for steady personal growth and develop a feeling of value and self-sympathy.

Sustaining Internal Exchange

Changing self-analysis includes supporting an empathetic inward discourse. PC emphasizes the significance of utilizing peaceful language and self-talk that is strong, empowering, and understanding. By supplanting self-decisive contemplations with kind and confirming proclamations, people can develop self-empathy and establish a seriously supporting interior climate.

Embracing Taking care of oneself

Taking care of oneself is an essential piece of self-sympathy. PC encourages people to focus on self-sustaining rehearsals that help their prosperity and feelings. Taking part in exercises that give pleasure, unwinding, and taking care of oneself encourages a feeling of empathy and self-association.

Care and Self-Reflection

Care and self-reflection are amazing assets for changing self-analysis. By developing a present-second mindfulness and noticing self-decisive considerations without judgment, people can foster a more noteworthy comprehension of their triggers and examples. Care takes into consideration an empathetic reaction to self-analysis, advancing self-acknowledgment and development.

Moving to a Development Mentality

Changing self-analysis includes moving towards a development mentality, which centers around learning, improvement, and versatility. PC gives important experiences and practices that can uphold this shift and cultivate a more humane and development situated way to deal with personal growth.

Embracing Slip-ups as Learning Amazing open doors

PC urges people to see botches as important learning open doors as opposed to private disappointments. By reexamining botches as venturing stones to development and improvement, people can move toward difficulties with interest, versatility, and a readiness to gain from their encounters.

Defining Reasonable Objectives

Changing self-analysis includes putting forth practical and feasible objectives. PC encourages people to lay out objectives that line up with their qualities, assets, and self-awareness. By laying out practical objectives, people can zero in on progress as opposed flawlessly, cultivating a mentality of self-acknowledgement and development.

Looking for Help and Cooperation

PC underscores the significance of association and coordinated effort. Changing self-analysis can be upheld by looking for help from confided in companions, guides, or advisors. Taking part in empathic discussions, sharing encounters, and getting approval and consolation from others can give a feeling of having a place and support self-sympathy.

Developing Appreciation and Appreciation

Appreciation and appreciation are strong remedies to self-analysis. PC encourages people to develop appreciation by zeroing in on their assets, achievements, and the positive parts of their lives. By rehearsing appreciation and valuing oneself, people can encourage self-empathy and develop a positive mental self view.

Changing self-analysis is an extraordinary cycle that requires mindfulness, self-sympathy, and a guarantee to self-awareness. By applying PC standards, people can move towards a more sympathetic and development situated mentality, cultivating self-acknowledgement, strength, and close to home prosperity. The excursion of changing self-analysis includes developing self-sympathy, sustaining an internal discourse of thoughtfulness and understanding, and embracing botches as any open doors for learning and development. By coordinating self-sympathy rehearses into day to day existence, people can establish a sustaining inside climate, improve their confidence, and encourage a positive work culture. In the accompanying sections, we will investigate extra parts of Peaceful Correspondence, including authority, sympathy building, and compromise, to further help self-improvement and sympathetic correspondence in the work environment.

CLOSE TO HOME PROSPERITY PRACTICES

Profound prosperity is a key part of carrying on with a satisfying and healthy lifestyle. With regards to quiet correspondence (PC), close to home prosperity rehearses include sustaining and really focusing on one's feelings, creating mindfulness, and developing techniques for overseeing and communicating feelings in sound and useful ways. In this section, we will investigate the idea of profound prosperity, its significance in private and expert life, and functional procedures and methods derived from PC standards to improve close to home prosperity.

Grasping Profound Prosperity

Close to home prosperity alludes to the capacity to comprehend, manage, and express feelings in a solid and adjusted way. It includes fostering a positive relationship with one's feelings, perceiving their significance, and finding proactive ways to help and really focus on them.

Feeling Mindfulness and Acknowledgment

Close to home prosperity begins with mindfulness and acknowledgment of one's feelings. PC emphasizes the significance of recognizing and embracing all feelings, it is viewed as trying or awkward to incorporate those that. By tolerating feelings without judgment, people can develop a more noteworthy comprehension of themselves and their close to home encounters.

Profound Guideline

Close to home guidelines are the capacity to successfully oversee and explore feelings. It includes perceiving and figuring out the triggers, examples, and power of one's feelings, and utilizing procedures to manage them in a sound and useful manner. PC offers methods to foster close to home guideline abilities, empowering people to answer their feelings with mindfulness and care.

Profound Articulation

Close to home prosperity incorporates the capacity to communicate feelings genuinely and emphatically. PC urges people to communicate their feelings sincerely and consciously, while likewise thinking about the effect of their appearance on others. Close to home articulation is a fundamental part of keeping up with sound connections and advancing open and empathic correspondence.

PROCEDURES FOR UPGRADING CLOSE TO HOME PROSPERITY

PC gives important procedures and practices that can improve profound prosperity and backing people in fostering a more amicable relationship with their feelings.

Self-Reflection and Mindfulness

Self-reflection and mindfulness are essential practices for upgrading close to home prosperity. PC accentuates the significance of self-reflection to develop comprehension of one's feelings, triggers, and needs. By participating in self-reflection rehearsals, for example, journaling or contemplation, people can develop mindfulness and gain bits of knowledge into their profound encounters.

Peaceful Self-Talk

PC urges people to take on peaceful self-talk while drawing in with their feelings. This includes utilizing empathetic and non-critical language to recognize and approve one's feelings. By rehearsing peaceful self-talk, people make a steady internal exchange that encourages self-acknowledgement and close to home prosperity.

Compassion for Self

Sympathy isn't just significant in connecting with others yet in addition in connecting with oneself. PC stresses the act of self-sympathy, which includes broadening grasping, empathy, and graciousness towards one's own feelings and requirements. By developing self-compassion, people can answer their own feelings with care and understanding, advancing profound prosperity.

Care and Profound Mindfulness

Care is a strong practice for upgrading close to home prosperity. By developing present-second mindfulness, people can notice their feelings without judgment, considering a more profound comprehension of their close to home scene. Care assists people with creating profound mindfulness and answering their feelings in a more deliberate and valuable manner.

CLOSE TO HOME PROSPERITY IN CONNECTIONS

Profound prosperity in connections is essential for encouraging grasping, compassion, and solid correspondence. PC gives experiences and practices that help profound prosperity in social settings.

Undivided attention and Empathic Comprehension

Undivided attention and empathic comprehension are fundamental for advancing close to home prosperity in connections. By mindfully standing by listening to others' feelings and needs and looking to comprehend their viewpoint, people can cultivate a more profound association and make a place of refuge for transparent close to home articulation.

Communicating Feelings Decisively

PCemphasizes the significance of communicating feelings self-assuredly and deferentially in connections. By communicating feelings sincerely and straightforwardly, people can convey their requirements and encounters while keeping up with compassion and thought for other people. Confident profound articulation upholds close to home prosperity by advancing comprehension and working with a solid goal of struggles.

Compromise with Sympathy

Profound prosperity is upheld by settling clashes in a caring and empathic way. PCoffers techniques for compromise that focus on getting it, compassion, and finding shared benefit arrangements. By moving toward clashes with compassion and a guarantee close to home prosperity, people can fabricate trust and reinforce their connections.

Developing Close to home Association

Profound prosperity is improved by developing profound association in connections. PC encourages people to participate in rehearsals that cultivate profound closeness, like sharing weak feelings, offering empathic reactions, and effectively looking for close to home association with others. Developing close to home association advances a feeling of having a place, backing, and generally profound prosperity.

Profound prosperity is fundamental for driving a reasonable and satisfying life. By consolidating PC principles and rehearses, people can upgrade their close to home prosperity by supporting a positive relationship with their feelings, creating mindfulness, and developing systems for overseeing and communicating feelings in solid and valuable ways. The excursion towards close to home prosperity includes self-reflection, self-compassion, care, and encouraging profound prosperity in connections. By focusing on close to home prosperity, people can work on their own and proficient connections, upgrade their general joy and fulfillment, and add to a positive and sustaining workplace. In the accompanying parts, we will investigate extra parts of Peaceful Correspondence, including authority, sympathy building, and compromise, to additional help close to home prosperity and humane correspondence in the working environment.

CONCLUSION

Peaceful correspondence (PC) offers an extraordinary way to deal with correspondence and connections, underscoring sympathy, understanding, and caring association. All through this book, we have investigated the standards, systems, and practices of PC, expecting to upgrade our relational abilities, resolve clashes, and develop agreeable connections. By incorporating PC standards into our lives, we can change the manner in which we connect with ourselves as well as other people, encouraging compassion, regard, and shared development.

Language significantly affects our connections, and through PC, we have taken in the significance of cognizant and peaceful language. By utilizing empathetic, legit, and non-critical words, we can make understanding, form trust, and advance open exchange. Our words hold the ability to extend association or make distance, and with PC, we have acquired the apparatuses to impart in manners that cultivate sympathy and association.

Sympathy has been a focal point of our investigation, as it is fundamental for significant associations. PC has shown us the worth of undivided attention, empathic comprehension, and viewpoint taking. By genuinely

147

hearing and grasping others' feelings, needs, and encounters, we establish a climate of acknowledgment, backing, and compassion. Through compassion, we overcome any barrier among ourselves as well as other people, advancing comprehension and supporting further associations.

Settling clashes with peacefulness has been one more center part of PC. By embracing compassion, undivided attention, and coordinated effort, we can find shared benefit arrangements that address the fundamental requirements of all gatherings included. Clashes become open doors for development, understanding, and innovative critical thinking. With PC, we have learned systems for changing contentions into valuable exchanges that extend understanding and encourage goals that honor everybody's necessities.

Trust and closeness are sustained through PC in our connections. By laying out shared objectives, advancing collaboration, and esteeming assorted viewpoints, we establish a climate of trust and security. Trust is based on unwavering quality, consistency, and respecting each other's viewpoints. PC teaches us to encourage further associations and engage people to communicate their thoughts legitimately, in this manner upgrading connections and advancing profound prosperity.

We have additionally investigated the utilization of PC in nurturing and the work environment. In nurturing, PC offers a sympathetic methodology that cultivates compassion, understanding, and profound improvement in youngsters. By building sympathy, settling clashes with empathy, and empowering close to home development, we develop solid and sound associations with our youngsters, furnishing them with the establishment for prosperity and self-improvement.

In the working environment, PC adds to powerful correspondence, compromise, and the production of a positive workplace. By incorporating PC principles, we advance open correspondence, joint effort, and regard. PC helps us to esteem different viewpoints, effectively tune in, and take part in genuine and empathic correspondence. Thus, we make a culture of shared help, efficiency, and prosperity.

PC has likewise directed us in developing self-empathy and changing self-analysis. By embracing self-acknowledgement, rehearsing self-empathy, and fostering a development mentality, we support a better relationship with ourselves. This improves our close to home prosperity and supports our capacity to take part in empathetic correspondence with others. Through self-sympathy, we recognize our humankind, embrace flaws, and develop benevolence and understanding towards ourselves.

All in all, peaceful correspondence offers a significant way to deal with correspondence and connections that can change our lives. By coordinating the standards and practices of PC, we can improve our capacity to speak with sympathy and understanding, resolve clashes in helpful ways, and develop amicable and significant connections. PC isn't simply a bunch of ideas, yet an approach to being — an approach to connecting with ourselves as well as other people with genuineness, sympathy, and empathy.

As we finish up this book, let us recollect that executing PC requires progressing practice, tolerance, and self-reflection. It is a deep rooted obligation to self-awareness, sympathy, and cognizant correspondence. By embracing the standards of PC and rehearsing them in our regular routines, we add to making an existence where sympathy and understanding win, clashes are settled with empathy, and correspondence turns into a vehicle for association and concordance.

May the illustrations and experiences acquired from this book guide us towards a more serene, caring, and agreeable world — a reality where our words and activities make waves of grasping, love, and positive change. Allow us to set out on this excursion of quiet correspondence together, embracing its groundbreaking power for ourselves, our connections, and our aggregate humankind.

Appendix: Communication Exercises and Practices

In this supplement, we will investigate an assortment of correspondence activities and practices that can additionally improve our comprehension and utilization of quiet correspondence (PC) standards. These activities are intended to extend our mindfulness, reinforce our empathic listening abilities, and develop humane correspondence in different settings. By participating in these activities, we can foster more prominent dominance of the PC and coordinate it all the more completely into our lives and connections.

1. Self-Reflection Activities:

Self-reflection is an important practice for creating mindfulness and acquiring bits of knowledge into our viewpoints, sentiments, and correspondence designs. The accompanying activities can uphold our excursion of self-disclosure and self-awareness:

- **Journaling:** Put away normal time for intelligent composition. Utilize your diary to investigate your feelings, needs, and encounters. Think about unambiguous circumstances and communications, looking at your viewpoints, sentiments, and the hidden necessities included.

- **Care Reflection:** Practice care contemplation to develop present-second mindfulness. Focus on your viewpoints, feelings, and real sensations without judgment. Notice any examples or triggers that emerge during your contemplation practice.

- **Values Appraisal:** Think about your own qualities and how they line up with your correspondence and relationship objectives. Recognize the qualities that are generally essential to you and consider how you can encapsulate them all the more completely in your connections.

2. Empathic Listening Activities:

Empathic listening is a basic expertise in PC that advances understanding and association. The accompanying activities can upgrade our capacity to tune in with compassion and make a place of refuge for others to articulate their thoughts:

- **Intelligent Tuning:** Practically speaking intelligent tuning in by rewording and summing up what others say. Center around understanding their viewpoint instead of planning your reaction. Focus on their feelings, needs, and the hidden message they are passing on.

- **Profound Tuning in:** Take part in profound tuning by concentrating on the speaker. Be available, keep in touch, and suspend judgment. Make a safe and non-critical space for the speaker to share their considerations and sentiments.

- **Compassion Circle:** Structure a little gathering and take part in sympathy circles. Every member alternates sharing their encounters while the others effectively tune in without intruding on or offering exhortation. The attention is on identifying understanding, instead of critical thinking.

3. Humane Correspondence Practices:

153

The accompanying practices are intended to encourage empathetic correspondence and compromise in different settings:

- **Quiet Correspondence Custom:** Make a day to day custom to set goals for caring correspondence. Take a couple of seconds every day to ponder your correspondence objectives and help yourself to remember the PC standards you need to epitomize.

- **Peaceful Language Challenge:** Set an individual test to kill brutal or critical language from your jargon. Supplant basic or accusing explanations with peaceful and humane language. Notice the effect this shift has on your correspondence and connections.

- **Pretending:** Participate in pretending activities to work on testing discussions or compromise situations. Alternate assuming various parts and examination with utilizing PC standards to direct your correspondence. Ponder the results and recognize regions for development.

- **Compassion Journalling:** notwithstanding private journaling, make a sympathy diary. Expound on circumstances where you rehearsed compassion and what it meant for your connections. Consider regions where you can extend your empathic abilities and set expectations for future development.

4. Joining into Day to day existence:

A definitive objective of PC is to incorporate its standards into our day to day routines. The accompanying practices can assist us with applying PC in certifiable circumstances:

- **Morning Goals:** Set aims for caring correspondence toward the start of every day. Consider how you need to appear in your collaborations and focus on rehearsing compassion, peaceful language, and aware tuning in.

- **Intelligent Respite:** Prior to answering in a discussion or during a possible struggle, take an intelligent delay. Think about the necessities and feelings at play, and express yourself and activities deliberately. This interruption permits you to answer as opposed to respond, advancing more humane and smart correspondence.

- **Appreciation and Appreciation:** Develop a day to day appreciation and appreciation practice. Set aside some margin to communicate appreciation for other people, recognizing their commitments and assets. This training encourages association and establishes a positive correspondence environment.

- **Empathetic Self-Talk:** Foster a propensity for sympathetic self-talk. Notice any self-decisive contemplations or decisions that emerge and deliberately supplant them with kind and steady articulations. Practice self-sympathy and recognize your endeavors in coordinating PC principles into your life.

By participating in these correspondence activities and practices, we can develop our comprehension and utilization of Peaceful Correspondence. As we keep on fostering our abilities, let us recollect that PC is a deep rooted excursion of development and learning. With persistence, commitment, and self-reflection, we can coordinate PCprinciples into our day to day routines, making a more caring and empathic approach to discussing and connecting with ourselves as well as other people.

Note: These activities and practices are expected as supplemental assets to help the standards and ideas talked about in this book. They are not comprehensive, and people are urged to investigate extra activities and adjust them to their interesting requirements and conditions.